Come
TO YOUR
Senses
(All eleven of them)

Design by Brian Bean
Edited by Jane Lind

Typeset by Attic Typesetting Inc.

Annick Press gratefully acknowledges the support of The Canada Council and the Ontario Arts Council.

The publisher shall not be liable for any damage which may be caused or sustained as a result of the conduct of any of the activities in this book, from not specifically following instructions or conducting the activities without proper supervision, or from ignoring the cautions contained in the text.

Canadian Cataloguing in Publication Data

Tytla, Milan.
Come to your senses

ISBN 1-55037-292-0

1. Senses and sensation—Juvenile literature
I. Title.

BF233.T88   1993   j152   C92-095468-5

Distributed in Canada by:
Firefly Books Ltd.
250 Sparks Avenue
Willowdale, Ontario
M2M 2S4 Canada

Distributed in the USA by:
Firefly Books (U.S.) Inc.
P.O. Box 1338,
Ellicott Station,
Buffalo, New York
14205   U.S.A.

Printed in Canada.

Come
TO YOUR
Senses
(All eleven of them)

Written by Milan Tytla

Illustrated by Chum Mcleod

ANNICK PRESS LTD.
TORONTO, ONTARIO

About the Author

Milan Tytla earned his Ph.D. in 1982 in Experimental Psychology, specializing in vision. Since then he has been Staff Scientist in the Departments of Ophthalmology, at The Hospital for Sick Children and at Toronto Hospital, and taught Perception at The University of Toronto. Milan has been interested in Perception since childhood. His first book, co-authored with Nancy Crystal, is entitled "You Won't Believe Your Eyes," and is all about the visual system.

Photo: Richard Milne

How to Use This Book

This book is about some of your senses—those parts of your body that your brain uses to explore the world and to discover how it works. To tell the complete story of the senses would require many volumes. So our aim is to help you discover, through experimentation, many of the remarkable abilities you employ to understand and decode the world around you. Count the number of senses you think you have. Seeing, hearing, tasting, smelling, and touching are the ones most people think of. But even the great thinker Aristotle, over 2000 years ago, figured out that there must be more than those five. For example, he knew that touch can be divided into the different feelings of temperature, pressure and pain. In this book you can experiment with eleven of your senses: taste, smell, pressure, hot, cold, muscle and joint, tilt, rotation (balance), sight and hearing. Single experiments or groups of them make terrific science projects, and you can connect and relate experiments using different senses. You can begin with any part of the book, and dive into each experiment. The book is fun to read, but there is even more fun in actually doing the experiments, especially with your friends. Except for a prism and some cheap tubing, the experiments require things you can find around your home. So . . . have fun as you Come To Your Senses!

Contents

Only
THE BEST OF
Taste

Taste Sense

Stick out your tongue and look at it in the mirror. Stick it way out. You are looking at 100 percent pure muscle wrapped in a skin. You use your tongue to move food around in your mouth while you are chewing. It helps when you swallow, and it is very useful when you talk. Of course, your tongue is also the organ of taste.

Take a really close look at your tongue's surface. It is covered in bumps, and you can see them even more clearly after swishing milk around in your mouth.

Those bumps are not your taste buds. Your taste buds are so tiny that you need a microscope or a very strong magnifying glass to see them. Taste buds line the sides of those bumps you see in the mirror.

Taste buds detect certain chemicals and send signals to the brain. The brain translates those signals into what we call taste. There are about 10,000 buds on the tongue and a few more in the mouth and throat. Before you can taste something, it has to dissolve in your saliva and come in contact with the taste buds. That is why your fork or glass is tasteless—steel and glass do not dissolve in saliva.

LET'S DO it!

Most scientists agree that there are four basic tastes—sweet, sour, salt, and bitter. Combinations of these produce other tastes. But as you will soon see, it is not that simple. You can begin by exploring your tongue.

What You Need

a friend with a tongue
cotton swabs twisted to a
    fine point
salt, sugar, white vinegar or
    pure lemon juice (sour),
    tonic water or caffeinated
    black coffee (bitter)
photocopy or tracing of the
    tongue picture
4 small glasses
4 pens or pencils of different
    colours
water (if your tap water has
    a taste, use *distilled*
    water, the kind your
    parents use in a steam
    iron)
measuring cup

What To Do

1 First, mix separate weak solutions of the four basic tastes. Start with four glasses each filled with about 125 mL of water. Stir a small amount of one of the substances in each glass and taste. Repeat, until you can slightly, but definitely, taste it.

2 Begin with the salty mixture by slightly dipping the pointed end of the swab into it. Then gently dab a tiny amount on some part of your friend's tongue.

Mark a dot on the tongue map if your friend tasted salt. Repeat until you have tested the whole tongue.

3 Repeat step 2 with the other three tastes, using a different coloured pen for each taste to mark the tongue map.

4 Every once in a while, let your friend take a break and rinse with plain water to refresh the tongue. Be careful when you dab close to the back of the tongue. Some people gag easily.

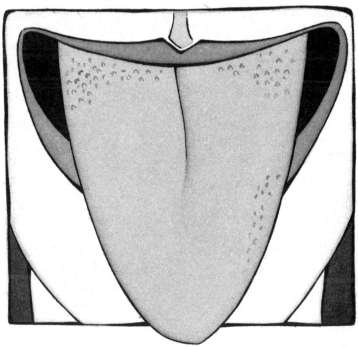

16

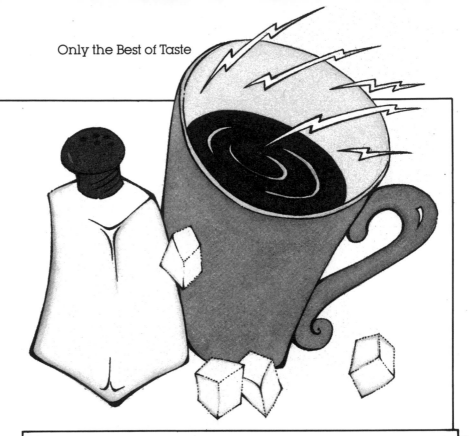

What did you discover? Is the middle of your tongue taste-blind? Good, it is supposed to be. There are no taste buds there. That is where food sits between being shovelled from one side of the mouth to the other when you chew. There are more taste buds around the edge and back of the tongue. In other words, many taste buds are close to the teeth, which cut the food and release more taste. The very tip of your tongue is most sensitive to salt. On either side of the salt area is where most of us taste sweet, and farther back still is the bitter. The taste of sour stands out along the sides of the tongue. These areas overlap a lot.

Notice that there are more of the different tastes at the tip of the tongue, the part we use when we just taste something. At the very back, close to your throat, is the bitter. So the back of the tongue is designed to do a final check for poisons before a person swallows — in the wild, poisonous things are often bitter. Did you find taste buds on the underside of your tongue?

GUESS What?

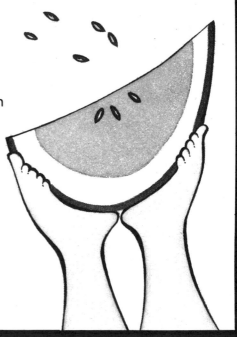

Not all creatures have taste buds on their tongues (in fact, not all creatures have tongues!). Many insects, such as the housefly and butterfly, have taste buds on their feet so they can taste as soon as they land and walk on food. Imagine tasting with your hands and feet! Fish, which are almost always underwater, have taste buds in their skin all over their bodies. Creatures also differ in the number of taste buds: chickens have only about 24, catfish have more than 175,000!

LET'S DO it!

Have you ever tasted a chocolate bar straight out of the freezer? It definitely did not have the rich taste it had before you put it in. What happened? Your sense of taste depends on many things. Temperature is one of them. Let's explore this idea.

What You Need

a friend
4 small glasses
sugar
salt
water (hot, warm and cold)
ice cubes
measuring cup

What To Do

1. Mix 5 mL of sugar in 65 mL of hot water and let it cool.

2. Place exactly 5 mL of this mixture into each glass. Number the glasses 1 to 4.

3. Add 65 mL of cold water to each of glasses 1 and 2, and add two ice cubes to glass 1.

4. Add 65 mL warm water to glass 3, and 65 mL hot water to glass 4.

5. Stir each mixture, but do not let your friend see what you are doing.

6. Ask your friend to sip each one and order the glasses from least to most sweet.

How did your friend do? Most people think the warm or hot mixture tastes the sweetest, and the ice-cold one the least sweet. The difference can be great. So, sweetness depends on

GUESS What?

Taste also depends on colour. Add some green or blue food colouring to milk and ask a friend to describe its taste (food colouring is tasteless). The food industry knows this very well and uses food dyes a lot to make foods look the way we expect them to. For example, most of us know that margarine is white but it is dyed to resemble butter. But did you know that uncoloured instant chocolate pudding can be a *martian green?* Look in your pantry or fridge to find prepared foods that have had colour added. "Naturally coloured" on the label does not have to mean that the colour came from anything you would normally call food. For example, a legal, natural, red food dye comes from a tiny female bug from South America called the coccus cacti (the dye is called cochineal), which is dried whole and powdered. And the shiny coating on many hard-shelled candies comes from the shells of beetles! Without knowing it, you probably eat mashed bugs regularly!

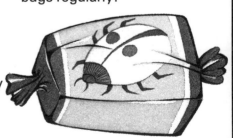

temperature. Do all the tastes?

Repeat the experiment with salt, bitter and sour. What you may discover is that saltiness is the opposite. Things taste the least salty when hot, and most salty when cold (try a hot dog or canned soup when it is hot, then cold).

Bitterness undergoes the same, but even greater, change that salt does (try hot and cold black coffee). Sourness is least affected by temperature—you may not even notice a difference. The temperature does not affect the amount of sugar, or salt, or whatever, in the mixture. Temperature changes the way your taste buds work.

GUESS
What?

The number of taste buds in your mouth changes throughout your life. When you were born, you had very few taste buds. Young children, on the other hand, have many more taste buds than adults. And adults lose more and more taste buds as they get older. This may explain why children and adults often do not like the same foods. Something spiced right for an adult might be overpowering for a child.

LET'S DO it!

The taste of something also depends on what you tasted just before. Water is probably the most tasteless stuff around. Distilled water has absolutely no taste because it is 100 percent pure and does not contain the chlorine and minerals in tap water. But we can make even distilled water have a taste without adding anything to it.

What You Need

1 tablespoon sugar dissolved in 125 mL water
1 tablespoon salt dissolved in 125 mL water
65 mL vinegar with 65 mL water
strong black coffee or tonic water
distilled water (the kind your parents use in a steam iron)
measuring cup and spoons

What To Do

1. Swirl one of the mixtures around in your mouth for 60 seconds.

2. Spit it out and immediately take a sip of distilled water.

3. Write down the taste of the water—it may be subtle, but it will be there.

4. Repeat with the other mixtures.

GUESS What?

Taste buds have a life span of less than ten days. That means that hundreds of taste buds are being replaced on your tongue right now as you read this paragraph, and all of them will be replaced by the time you finish this book.

What did you discover? That even distilled water can have a taste? Was it sweet after rinsing with the sour vinegar or bitter coffee? Was it sour or bitter after salt or sweet? You experienced an aftereffect—one substance had an effect on the taste of the substance after it.

This is what happened. During the 60 seconds of swirling with salt, only your salt taste buds are signalling, but they soon get tired and for a short time afterward cannot send any signals. When you then taste the water, your brain is not getting the usual balanced signal from all the taste buds and assumes the water must have some taste. While we are eating, this kind of aftereffect must be happening all the time, always subtly changing the taste of the food with each new bite.

DID YOU EVER
Wonder?

Why does orange juice taste so horrible after you have just brushed your teeth? Toothpaste is ground-up chalk and other powders that taste terrible by themselves. The makers of toothpaste add artificial flavours and sweeteners. The sweetness would stay in your mouth for a long time after brushing and would soon become unpleasant, so the toothpaste makers also add something to the toothpaste that shuts off the sweet taste buds for quite some time after brushing. When you drink your juice, the only taste buds working are those that can pick up the sour and bitter tastes that are also part of the juice. Next time, brush *after* breakfast!

LET'S DO it!

Find out how much smell affects what you taste.

A large part of what we call taste is influenced by smell. In fact, most scientists think that only a tiny part of tasting comes from our taste buds. Smell is the main part of tasting.

What You Need

a friend
small cube of a peeled apple, potato, and onion, all fresh, crisp and juicy
swimmer's nose plugs that permit no air (or hold your nose with your fingers)
good blindfold

What To Do

1. Block your nostrils completely. You should not be able to smell anything or breath through your nose.

DID YOU EVER Wonder?

Do you have a strong dislike for a food that most people like and that you liked when you were younger? Just the smell of it makes you queasy and nearly throw up? There is a good chance you have a "learned taste aversion." That is a dislike for food that you learned. Many people have them. What happened was that at some time you became very ill, say with a flu, within hours of eating a particular food. Your brain assumed that that food made you ill and therefore stopped you from tasting it for years to come! Obviously, this process would be important if you were really poisoned. But this time you made a wrong guess. The reason rats and mice are so difficult to exterminate is probably because this process is extremely strong in their brains. If a rodent tasted a poisoned food that was enough to cause illness but not death, that rodent will never touch that food for the rest of its life!

2 Put on the blindfold and make sure you cannot see out the bottom.

3 Have your friend give you one of the three food cubes to chew. What did you taste? Repeat with the other two foods.

4 Repeat step 3 with your nose unplugged but still blindfolded. Then let your friend try.

Is it not surprising how poor your sense of taste is when your sense of smell is taken away? By the way, these foods make good samples because they are close in texture and moisture—two other cues to taste. When you have a cold your sense of smell is sometimes totally blocked, and food loses much of its flavour. All you can taste then are the basics provided by the taste buds—sweet, sour, salt and bitter. When you did the experiment, did you notice that when you added *smell, taste* increased, not smell? Can you guess what would happen if you bit and chewed the potato while you steadily smelled the apple? Try it.

DID YOU EVER
Wonder?

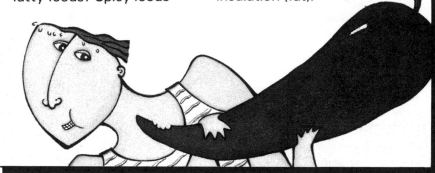

Why do people who live around the equator, in hot countries, eat spicy, hot foods, whereas people living closer to the North and South Poles eat more bland, fatty foods? Spicy foods make you sweat, and when the sweat evaporates, it cools you down! People close to the poles eat fatty foods, which their bodies burn for heat or store for insulation (fat).

A great many common, everyday foods are nearly impossible to taste when you are unable to smell them. Repeat the experiment with other friends and use the foods in List A and List B. To identify List A foods you need your sense of smell. You can identify List B foods more easily without smell. If you want to design a truly accurate experiment, mash or mince each food with a tiny bit of water so that texture and moisture do not give away the tastes of the foods. Have each friend whisper the answer into your ear and record if it is correct (so that the other tasters will not be influenced).

List A	List B
Coffee	Vinegar
Cherry	Lemon
Molasses	Onion
Garlic	Water
Apricot	Grape Juice
Pineapple	Cheese
Root Beer	Ketchup
Chocolate	Worcestershire
Cranberry	Sauce
Juice	Grapes
Pickle Juice	Mustard

THE
Nose
Knows

Smell Sense

Take a long, deep sniff through your nose to smell a flower, a chocolate bar, a double-decker cheeseburger, or a deep-dish pizza. You are using your two nostrils to take in air that holds chemicals from these things. The air swirls around the baffles in your two nasal cavities, and hits your smell cells lining the ceiling of each cavity. From the picture, you can see that your nose and mouth are joined. So, smells can also get to the smell cells from your mouth by breathing through your mouth, or from food you are chewing, or by burping.

At the very top of each nasal cavity, you have about 5 million smell cells, each grouped in a thin patch of 2 to

GUESS
What?

There have been at least 30 different ideas about how the smell sense works. The lock-and-key idea was first thought up by a Greek *poet*, named Lucretius, over 2000 years ago.

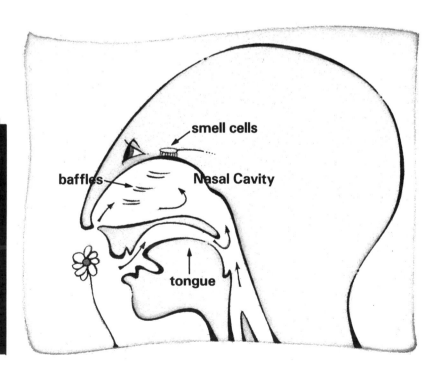

smell cells

baffles

Nasal Cavity

tongue

2.5 cm around. This may sound like a lot, but dogs, for example, have about 100 million per nostril. This difference probably explains why hounds can sniff and follow the track of someone hours after he or she has disappeared. Even the smell left *by only a fingerprint* is enough for these hounds!

Smell, like taste, is a chemical sense. To be "smell-able," molecules, which are tiny pieces of matter, must travel in the air, either in evaporation, or in a fine dust or powder. When these molecules touch the hairs of the smell cells, they send smell signals to the brain, which figures out the type of smell. If you smell smoke or bad fumes, your brain senses danger. If milk has gone bad, your sense of smell warns you. And if you smell a lily, or spaghetti sauce cooking, you can just enjoy it.

Different types of smell cells detect and give a signal of basic smells. Different mixtures of these signals make up the many different smells. Scientists think that for humans there are probably seven main smelly chemicals, and the molecules of each have a unique shape. And on the smell cells there are unique "pores" into which the

molecules fit—somewhat like a lock and key. The smell cells have seven different locks and each chemical is one of the seven different keys. If a key fits one of the locks, the cells signal that chemical. If there is no lock for the chemical key, you cannot smell it. For example, we do not have a lock

for sugar, and pure sugar by itself has no smell. There are also a few cells, called free nerve endings, that give a "feeling" to certain smells. The burn of ammonia or hot peppers, the coolness of mint or menthol, or the tingling you feel when you burp cola are examples.

The seven primary smells are:

Primary Odor	Example
Camphoric	Moth Balls
Musky	Musk Perfume/After-shave
Floral	Roses
Pepperminty	Mint Candy
Ethereal	Dry Cleaning Fluid
Pungent	Vinegar
Putrid	Rotten Egg

We humans usually rely on our sense of vision (and hearing) to identify things. For example, you know an apple because it is roundish, shiny, red or green, and has a stem on top. You do not need to

smell it before eating (unless you suspect it is plastic). You already know that taste depends on many things, especially smell. Does your sense of smell depend on anything else?

LET'S DO it!

Does smell depend on vision? How good are you at recognizing smells when you are blindfolded?

What You Need

At least 12 smelly things that you have smelled before. Use your imagination for ideas of things to smell. For example: pickle juice, coffee, sawdust, mashed green leaf, pencil shavings, cinnamon, ginger, vanilla, cheese, onion, garlic, ashes, cigar, ham, chocolate

jars or plastic containers with tight lids

several friends

pen and paper for each person

What To Do

1 Put each smelly thing in its own labelled container and seal it. Number the containers. Hide all of them in a bag. Give each friend a pen and piece of paper with the person's name and a list of numbers, one for each of the smells.

2 Ask your friends to tightly close their eyes. Have them each sniff one of the mystery smells. Call out the number on the container and ask everyone to write down in secret beside the number what they each think the smell is. If they cannot name it, but they know they have smelled it before, have them just write a check mark. If they do not have a clue, write an X. Put the finished mystery smell back in the container.

GUESS What?

Pure natural gas is completely odorless. So why does it smell like rotten cabbage? Natural gas is very dangerous in two different ways: 1) it is toxic to breathe, and 2) it is extremely flammable and explosive. A leak of pure natural gas would go totally unnoticed until too late. A stinky chemical is added to the gas so we can detect the leak. This chemical was chosen because, not only does it have a distinct stink, but we are also *extremely* sensitive to it — 1 molecule of it in 50 billion molecules of air is enough to smell it!

3 Repeat step 2 until all the smells are done.

4 Collect the score sheets.

What did you discover? How many things that seemed familiar did everyone miss (check marks)? This is called the "tip-of-the-nose" phenomenon (like the tip-of-the-tongue phenomenon when you know the word but can't seem to find it). Pick out someone's score sheet and have that person sniff some of the "checked" smells again with eyes closed. But now give the sniffer a hint. For example, say "cucumber," "dill," or the brand name of the pickle juice. The sniffer will probably now recognize it. So, the sense of smell is helped by another sense — hearing. And, of course, vision would really help: see how few errors your sniffers make with eyes open.

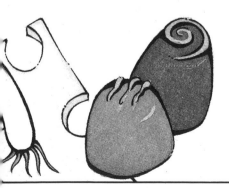

GUESS What?

You probably know that many creatures communicate by smell. They produce chemicals called pheromones (FER-uh-moans) which can signal danger, fear, anger, where food is, and where a mate is. A skunk's spray, for example, definitely signals "warning." Insects, especially, rely on this communication. The huge column of ants leading from the anthill to your picnic is following a pheromone trail laid down by the first ant to find your food.

Humans use pheromones to control insect pests. For example, the active ingredient in many insect repellants — citronellal — is a manufactured pheromone that copies the alarm signal. Mosquitos stay away, not because you stink but because your smell seems dangerous! And many harmful insect pests are being tricked into traps which have attractive pheromones. Scientists are not yet sure if humans use pheromones to communicate. But some moms can almost always tell which T-shirt belongs to their own child when jumbled with other kids' shirts, and can even tell brothers' or sisters' shirts apart, with just a sniff.

LET'S DO it!

For this next demonstration, we will dive straight into the experiment and discuss it later. Do not read it through first; just do exactly what it says step by step.

What You **Need**

something with a strong smell: soap, slice of onion, ground coffee, after-shave

What To **Do**

1. Pinch shut *one* nostril completely so you cannot breathe through it.

2. Hold the smelly thing under your nose right now.

3. Keep it there while you read.

Adaptation means getting used to something. As you adapt you become less sensitive—the smell fades. You are going to find out if your sense of smell adapts and if it does, where this happens—in your nose or in your brain.

You probably have experienced smell adaptation before. Remember the last time you were in a stinky barn or at the zoo or a fair and the animal smells became less strong the longer you stayed?

The same thing is happening right now. You will notice that whatever you have been sniffing all this time is not as strong as it was in the beginning. In other words, you are adapting to the smell. That is the answer to the first question (but keep on sniffing).

Now tackle the second question: where does adaptation happen? Your two nasal cavities behind each nostril are totally separate, and the smell cells in each send separate

DID YOU EVER Wonder?

Why does one nostril seem to breathe more than the other? Actually, your nostrils take turns breathing. About every two to three hours the lining of one nostril swells and closes a bit while the other opens. Check out this nasal cycle by exhaling out your nose onto a pocket mirror held directly under it. Notice how one condensation circle is larger than the other? Repeat in about 2.5 hours. Did they switch?

messages to the brain where the two signals are combined. If adaptation is happening within the smell cells themselves, then only the cells behind the unplugged nostril should have adapted—the cells behind the plugged nostril should be fresh and unadapted. *Now read the next paragraph. Then do what it says.*

Quickly take your finger off your nostril and pinch the other nostril shut with your finger. Sniff with your fresh, unadapted nostril. Compare how strong the smell is to the two nostrils. The strength of the smelly thing is probably the same in both nostrils. In other words, the other nostril adapted without smelling. The only way this could have happened is if the *smell centre in the brain* adapted, the centre where cells from both nostrils send their signals. Something else you should notice is that when you have adapted, not all smells are dulled, but instead, only the smell to which you had adapted is dulled. For example, if you adapted to an onion, the smell of perfume or skunk would be as strong as usual.

GUESS What?

Doctors can diagnose an illness by the smell of your breath. For example, the smell of peanuts may mean a child has swallowed rat poison, and arsenic poisoning creates a garlic smell; yellow fever smells like raw meat; diabetes smells like sweet apples; and people with kidney failure smell of ammonia. The list is quite long. These clues are especially useful if the patient is unconscious, but of course the smell of peanuts or garlic might also simply mean that the child just ate a peanut butter sandwich or pizza.

Tongue Twister:
Say "smell cell" quickly ten times in a row!!!

A Touching Experience

Skin, Muscle and Joint Senses

Find a tennis ball (or a peach), and go to the fridge and get an egg. Sit down, and with your eyes closed, handle and feel these two objects. Pay close attention to all the sensations you feel, and all the descriptions you can make. You will notice right away how the two objects differ in temperature and in texture (smooth or rough). The tennis ball is neither warm nor cold, but the egg is definitely cold. The ball is fuzzy and rough, and the egg is smooth with tiny dimples on its surface.

These two sensations—temperature and pressure (texture is really the feeling of pressure on different parts of the skin)—belong to what we call "touch," which is the sense of the skin. Most scientists also add pain to the touch list. We'll

find out about these soon. But first concentrate on all the other information you can get from the egg and ball using only your hand.

You can easily tell that they differ in weight. They also differ in size, shape, and hardness. And the ball seems light for its size and the egg seems heavy for its size, so you probably correctly guessed

that the tennis ball is hollow, and the egg, filled.

Except for temperature, texture and weight, the other sensations do not come from the skin. Prove it to yourself. Lay your outstretched hand, palm up, on a table. Have a friend gently place the ball or egg on your palm. Keep your eyes closed and do not move a muscle! Except for

temperature, texture and weight, you cannot tell anything else about the object. And if you keep perfectly still, even the fuzziness of the tennis ball disappears.

Where was the other information coming from, if not from the skin? I gave you a hint a few sentences back; do not move a muscle.

Try this: with your eyes tightly closed, touch the tip of your finger to the tip of your nose. You can do this because you have senses in your muscles and joints (body senses) that tell how much force you are applying, and the position of your bones. So, for example, to tell that the egg is hard, your brain has to know how much pressure is on the skin of your fingertips. It also has to know how hard your muscles are working to create that pressure. If you push hard and there is lots of pressure, your brain says "hard." If you push lightly, and there is little pressure, it must be "mushy" (like the inside of the egg if you pushed too hard). Notice that the skin and body senses cooperate similar to the way taste and smell do, when smelling what you eat greatly changes its taste. You successfully touched your nose because your brain knows where your nose is. Also, by knowing what your muscles and joints are doing, your brain guided your arm to the target.

Skin Senses

The human body can work in only a small range of temperature. Your normal inside temperature is about 37°C and if it goes above 41°C or below 33°C you will become unconscious. Your outside skin temperature is around 33°C. If it gets too cold, you could freeze, and you have to do something about it. To warm up you can shiver, exercise, build a fire, put on more clothing, or move to where it is warmer—indoors or toward the equator. If you get too hot, you will cook and dry up, so to cool down you sweat, calm down, remove clothing, turn on the fan or air conditioner, or move to where it is cooler— into a lake or pool or away from the equator.

Your body does a wonderful job of keeping your temperature steady. You have sense cells that monitor temperature, but no one has yet found them in a human body. This diagram shows a magnified slice of skin from

Chunk of Palm Skin

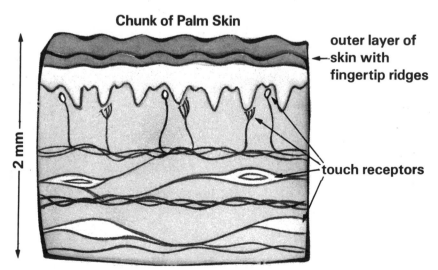

outer layer of skin with fingertip ridges

2 mm

touch receptors

the palm of the hand and the types of sense cells there are. These cells all seem to signal pressure—not temperature. It might be that groups of cells signal temperature. Scientists *do know* that there must be separate detector cells for hot

and for cold—not just one cell that measures temperature as a thermometer does. There are tiny areas on the skin that will always report hot if touched by a hot *or cold* needle. There are also cold spots, and they never overlap with hot spots. Have you ever had this experience: a single drop of water from a boiling pot of water splashes on your hand and feels ice cold, yet you know that the water is very hot! That tiny drop probably fell only on a single cold spot, which could report only "cold."

GUESS What?

Although scientists are not yet sure which skin cells are the temperature detectors, one possibility is a class of cells called "free-nerve endings," which are found all over the body. They got one hint from pit vipers,

snakes that have pits with only free-nerve endings in their head. The snakes use these pits to zero in on the heat produced by warm, tasty little mammals such as mice.

LET'S DO it!

Your hot and cold detectors do a fantastic job of controlling your body temperature. But they do not measure *real* temperature! In other words, they would not make good thermometers. Find out about your hot and cold detectors in the next two experiments.

What You Need

metal spoon
plastic spoon
wooden spoon
teddy bear
hot water

What To Do

Place these objects together on a wooden table or carpet for one hour, out of direct sunlight, and away from a heating or cooling vent.

Experiment A   When the hour is up, touch the underside of your forearm (the hairless side) with each of these objects and order them from coldest to warmest.

Experiment B   Touch different parts of your body with the metal spoon and find where the feeling of cold is the most and least noticeable. Use several metal spoons in order, so you have a fresh cold one each time. Repeat the experiment, using several spoons kept in hot water. Dry the spoon before touching and put it back in the water afterwards.

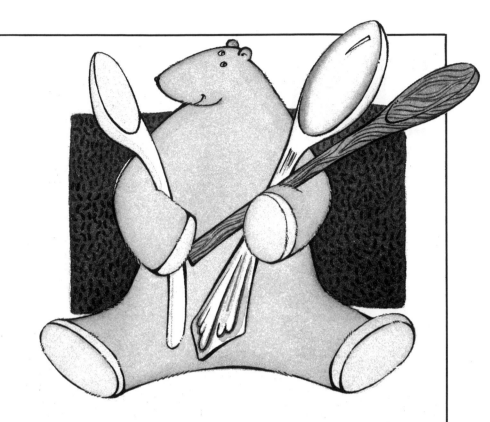

In Experiment A, you likely ordered the spoons the way they are listed, with the metal spoon being the coldest. But they are all really the *exact same temperature* if you left them in the same place for an hour. What are your detectors detecting? They are detecting *change* of temperature. Metal and plastic are good conductors of heat; they draw heat away from you rapidly, and feel cold. The wooden spoon and the teddy bear are not good conductors of heat, and feel warmer. So now you know why a tiled floor feels so much colder to your feet than a carpet. They can be the same temperature, but tiles are good conductors of heat, and fabric is not.

In Experiment B you probably discovered that different parts of your body have different sensitivities to temperature. Your forehead is sensitive to heat, and your lower leg is not very sensitive. You probably also discovered that being sensitive to heat does not mean you are also sensitive to cold in the same spot. For example, your forehead is not very sensitive to cold, but your chest and belly are. (Remember how, in the middle of the winter, you were hardly bothered by your bare forehead outdoors, but how you jumped when the doctor touched your chest with a stethoscope, which was at room temperature?) You probably have many hot detectors, but few cold detectors in the skin of your forehead.

LET'S DO it!

The temperature of your skin affects how warm or cold something feels. Your earlobes are one of the coldest body parts—27°C—because the small amount of blood in them moves slowly, and they dangle in the air. Hold one between your fingers and notice that your fingers feel warm to your lobe but that your lobe feels cold to your fingers. Check it out another way.

What You Need

2 bowls large enough to
    contain one hand each
1 bowl large enough to
    contain both hands
hot and cold water

What To Do

1. Fill both smaller bowls with comfortably hot water, and empty one into the larger bowl.

2. Refill the empty bowl with cold water and empty it into the large bowl. Refill the small bowl with cold water.

3. Arrange the bowls in a line in front of you with the lukewarm water in the middle. Place one hand in the hot water, and the other in the cold water. Keep them there for at least three minutes.

4. Quickly place both hands into the lukewarm water and feel its temperature.

Did the lukewarm water feel cold to the heated hand but warm to the chilled hand? But how can this be if the temperature of the water in the big bowl is the same all over? Each hand got used to (adapted to) the temperature of the hot and cold water in

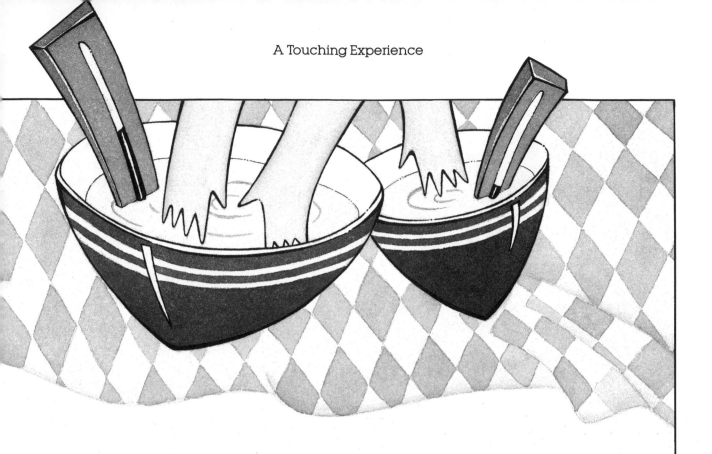

the two bowls. So, the hand in hot water became less sensitive to heat while it was adapting, and needed more heat than usual to be able to feel it. You might have noticed that the hot water seemed less and less hot during adaptation. When you put this hand into the lukewarm water, it could not feel the little heat that was in it. Adaptation explains why, when you first jump into the lake, it seems ice cold, but after splashing around for a few minutes, it becomes very comfortable. Your skin adapts to the cool water and becomes less sensitive to it.

GUESS What?

How heavy something feels on your skin depends on its temperature. Find two identical coins, say, two quarters. These quarters are exactly the same weight— convince yourself by placing both, a few inches apart, on the skin of your forearm (palm up). Now place one quarter on ice for five minutes and keep the other one at room temperature. Quickly dry off the cool coin and replace both on your forearm. Does the cool coin

seem heavier than the other? Scientists do not completely understand this effect, but they think it shows that the receptors designed to feel pressure may also feel temperature.

LET'S DO it!

The feeling of pressure or touch by the skin is fairly well understood. Those four types of skin receptors shown on page 31 each become excited and send a signal to the brain if they are stretched, bent or squeezed (which is what happens when the skin is pressed). These are probably the touch receptors.

Our sense of touch can be extremely fine. In other words, we can tell when two points are separated by very tiny distances. This kind of measure is called acuity—how close two points can be before they blend into each other and seem like one point. But as you will discover in this experiment, your acuity is vastly different at different places on your body.

What You Need

a blindfolded friend
compass (the circle-drawing kind), or 2 toothpicks and a ball of fairly hard putty or plasticine
ruler

What To Do

1 If you cannot find a compass, make one by sticking the blunt ends of both toothpicks close together into the putty.

You can move the two sharp ends toward and away from each other and they will hold that position like a compass.

2 Use the ruler to separate the ends of your compass by exactly 4 cm.

3 Then blindfold your friend and gently touch his or her lip, hand and shoulder with both points (try to touch both at the same time).

4 At each touch point your friend will report if she felt one or two points.

5 Now cut the distance between the points in half, and go to step 3.

6 Every once in a while, to keep your friend on his toes, touch with just one point.

7 Repeat until your friend feels only one point at each of the three places all the time.

What did you discover about touch acuity? You probably found out that the points could be quite far apart on the shoulder but they feel like one point (maybe up to 1 cm apart). But on the lips, you may not have been able to get the points close enough to seem like one — many people can detect points that are only 2 mm apart on the lips! In other words, the acuity of your lips is much finer than your shoulders, and your hand is somewhere in between. Measure the acuity of your skin on other parts of your body. Your back is particularly poor at this task.

DID YOU EVER
Wonder?

In the movies, we often see robbers filing or sanding their fingertips before cracking open a safe, presumably to give them a finer sense of touch. Is there any truth to this? I could not find any burglars to check this out with, but scientist Susan Lederman of Queen's University thinks it probably does help. Safecrackers feel for tiny spots of roughness when turning the dial of the combination lock. Dr. Lederman found that our ability to feel roughness depends on the thickness of callus (the thickened, dead outermost layer of skin) on our fingertips. Your index (pointing) fingertip, for example, has the thickest callus, and your ring finger the thinnest, and she discovered that the index finger really is poorer at feeling roughness than the ring finger. You can check this out for yourself by feeling the roughness of a friend's cheek or some cloth with each of these fingers. They should feel rougher to the more sensitive ring finger.

Crossing Your Fingers (and Getting Your Signals Crossed)

Usually we can easily locate where on the body we have been touched. For example, if someone gently poked you with a finger in several places, you would know exactly where, and that it was with one finger only. Over 2000 years ago, a famous great thinker, Aristotle, discovered that this is not always so.

Fool your friends with this simple demonstration. Have your friend, whose eyes are closed, place his or her crossed fingers at the edge of a table, as in the diagram (cross them as much as possible). Now gently but firmly touch both fingertips at the same time with the blunt end of a pencil. Ask how many things touched him. He will say two! Can you figure out why he made this silly error? Think about it; you actually touched him on the outsides of the crossed fingers. When your fingers are uncrossed, what would normally cause those two spots to be touched at the same time? Two separate things! It seems that your mind did not take into account that the fingers were crossed!

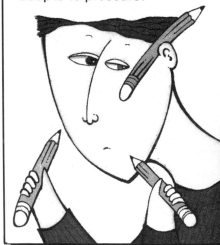

GUESS What?

How often have you searched all over the house for a pencil or eyeglasses only to realize that your pencil is behind your ear and that your glasses are on your nose! This is a comical example of how your skin adapts to pressure.

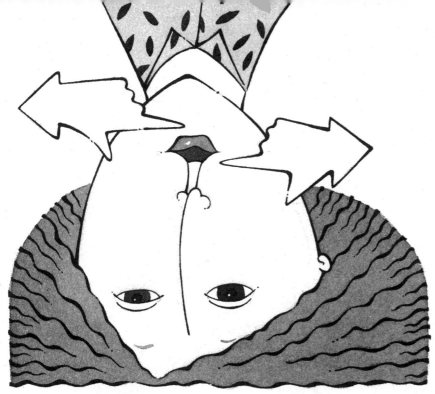

up and down, not slanted to either side, and ask her if the card is straight up and down, or slanted (do not touch her fingers). Tell her to open her eyes and watch her surprise! By looking back to Aristotle's demonstration, you should now be able to figure out how this lip illusion works.

These last two demonstrations tell us something about the body—it has a "touch" map. Normally we can tell where we are being touched because the mind has a map of every tiny place on our skin. Crossing your fingers or twisting your lips rearranged the touch map so that those patches of skin were in new, different places, but your mind used the old map—the only one it knows—and chose the old, wrong places.

Your mind actually has many maps of your body. Remember how you could successfully touch your finger to your nose blindfolded? The information for this map comes from sense cells in the muscles and joints, which respond to stretching. The scientific name for this sense is kinesthesis (kih-ness-THEEE-sis), but let's just call it the body sense, and its map the body map.

This next demonstration is similar, but even more weird. Have your friend place her right index finger above her upper lip and her left index finger below her lower lip (see diagram). Gently, but firmly have her pull her fingers apart to hold the lips in that slant (left finger pulls left, right pulls right) and ask her to close her eyes. Now you touch the centre of her lips with the corner of a card held straight

LET'S DO it!

Your touch map and your body map work very closely together. In fact, a lot of what we call "touch" really comes from the body sense. Do this simple experiment and you might be surprised at how poor the sense of touch is by itself.

What You Need

several friends
as many cookie cutters as you can find or borrow (8 to 10 is a good number)

What To Do

1. Fully blindfold yourself and place your hand flat on a table, palm side up.

2. Have a friend gently press a cookie cutter onto your palm. Leave it there for ten seconds, then remove it. During this time **you must not move a muscle** in your hand.

3. Your job is to identify the shape.

4. Repeat with all the other shapes, and keep a count of the number of correct answers.

5. Now, with the blindfold still in place, repeat the experiment, but this time have the friend just place the cookie cutter in your hand, and explore it with your fingers and hand. Keep a count of correct answers.

6. Try it on your friends.

Were you surprised at how few shapes you could recognize when you could not move your hand? In other words, without the body sense in our hand, the

touch sense by itself was really quite poor at identifying shapes. But when you were allowed to explore—in other words, add information from your muscles and joints—you were able to identify most or all shapes. So when we are actively touching something, we really are using many different senses.

GUESS
What?

There are a few rare people who do not have kinesthesis—the body sense. It can be lost in certain parts of the body because of illness or injury. There is a true story of a young mother who had no body sense in her right arm, and could only hold it in a certain position, or move it somewhere, by using her vision to guide it. Once, when holding her baby, she made the mistake of turning her head to the side. Not looking at her arm, she dropped the baby. Fortunately, the baby was O.K.!

LET'S DO it!

One very interesting thing about our touch and body maps is that they are forever changing. Why? The answer is easy: because our body's size and shape changes throughout our lives. We grow rapidly from birth, become fatter or skinnier, and then shrink with old age. No single map could work. We have to relearn a new map regularly; otherwise, we would never know where our parts are!

In this next experiment, you are going to change your body map, but before you try it, you need to know about one more map. This one is simple—it is the visual map of your body and where its parts are in comparison to your surroundings.

Imagine this: you want to pass through a doorway. As you walk toward the closed door, your vision is guiding you to it and your body sense is telling your brain where your legs are and what they are doing so it can send the correct signals to get you there. Vision tells your brain where the door handle is, and your brain signals the arm to exactly that place. You do not miss the handle because your vision map and your body map are the same. *Where you see* the handle is where you send your hand and *where you feel* the handle to be. Vision is also directly guiding your hand by showing you the shrinking distance between your hand and the handle. Now let's start the experiment!

What You Need

friends
a prism (perhaps you can
    borrow one from school)
cheap plastic safety or
    diving goggles (the ones
    that wrap completely
    around the eyes)
masking tape

What To Do

1. Put the goggles on and have an adult arrange the prism on one of the lenses of the goggles so that it is exactly in front of one eye (your favourite eye) when you are looking straight forward, and its bottom is horizontal (parallel with the ground). Carefully tape the prism in place without covering its front. See the diagram. The base of the prism (the wide end) can go to the left or right.

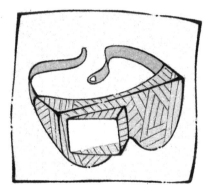

2. Cover every bit of the outside of the goggles and sides of the prism (but not its front) with masking tape. You should only be able to see through the prism with one eye. You have just made prism goggles.
Have a friend read the rest of the instructions to you as you carry them out.

3 Without the goggles on, ask your friend to hold up one flat hand with the palm facing you. Stand in front of your friend at exactly your arm's length from the hand.

4 Hold your favourite hand at your side and then use it to quickly punch his hand. Drop your hand back to your side. Do this several times to convince yourself and your friend that you can hit it (to show that your vision map and your body map line up exactly). From now on you will use only that same hand.

5 Nobody changes position, but you put the goggles on and immediately drop your hands to your sides.

6 Quickly punch his hand once and drop your hand. What happened?

7 Punch his hand ten times quickly. What is happening?

8 Once you are back to hitting his hand, hit it another ten times to be sure.

9 **Just once,** punch with your other hand. What happened?

10 Quickly remove the goggles and immediately punch his hand with your favourite hand. What happened this time?

As you quickly discovered, the prism shifted the images going into your eye to the left or right (depending on which way you angled the prism). This is very interesting because now your visual map and your body map do not line up as they used to. What was straight ahead according to your new vision map was not straight ahead according to your body map. That is exactly why, with goggles on, you missed the first punch in step 6. Where you saw the target was not where it really was, but your body map did not know this. As you continued to punch you got closer and closer to hitting. Something was changing—your visual and body maps were coming back together! (You will see which map did the changing in a moment.) With the two maps now lined up again, when you removed the goggles, you missed in the opposite direction. But of course you should have! This new alignment between the two maps was now incorrect, and you had to relearn the new relationship.

What changed? Did your vision map slide over to the body map or did the body map shift over to fit the vision map? Actually, you already have the answer (Hint: step 9). If your vision map changed, then after the learning period with your favourite hand, your other hand (or any other part of your body) should not have missed either. But it did. In fact, any other part of your body would have missed, because you learned to point your favourite hand (and its arm) in a new direction.

Notice how quickly your body map was learned and relearned—in just a few minutes! This is a very adaptable system. Try this on other friends; they will be totally amazed. Spend about a half hour doing something with the goggles that involves your hands and eyes—like a board game, or a jigsaw puzzle. Then see how long it takes you to relearn after removing the goggles. Reach for the door handle or a friend's hand, for example. If you are really adventurous, try a friendly game of ping pong or catch, first with, then without, the goggles. You will be amazed, especially when you play without goggles after a full game with goggles!

DID YOU EVER
Wonder?

Why do you feel pain? For example, what is the point in feeling deep and sharp pain after gashing your knee when you can see by the shredded skin and blood that your knee is injured and needs attention? There are at least two reasons why pain really is a good thing. First, what if you did not see the gash and just went along your merry way? You could bleed to death or get a fatal infection. Also, some sources of pain are always invisible—those inside your body. Second, pain teaches us to avoid those places or activities that are dangerous and harmful. Some people are born without the pain sensation. You might think they are lucky! They really are not. They usually do not live very long for exactly these reasons!

44

THE
Balancing Act

Vestibular Sense

Stand a pencil on its end, straight up and down, then let go. What happened? The pencil fell over, of course. When you stand up straight, why don't *you* fall over like the pencil? Because people have a sense of balance; pencils do not. Have you ever watched people or yourself in a crowd, especially during the playing of the national anthem or during prayer? Notice how you sway slightly back and forth. This is your balance sense detecting that you are tipping off-centre and the brain sending signals to the proper muscles to straighten you up. What information do we use to balance? Basically, it is gravity, and the direction it is pulling from. In other words, we detect *DOWN*.

We use many senses in balancing. One is vision. For instance, we know that trees and buildings are generally straight up and down; we know where the ground should be, and that water pours down. A quick look around tells us immediately where down is. But we can obviously still balance without vision. Totally blind people do not fall over. Convince yourself by standing up straight and closing your eyes. You will not fall over, but notice that with your eyes

closed, you sway more than when they are open. So vision does help.

Sometimes vision can be overpowering. If you have ever experienced a wild airplane or roller-coaster ride in a wide-screen movie—Canada's IMAX—you can be totally convinced that you and not the film are moving and tilting.

Touch is another sense that tells you where down is. As you sit reading this book, the pressure senses in your bottom and your feet are signalling to your brain, and it assumes that is because of gravity pulling you down.

GUESS What?

A simulated space ride at Disney World in Florida uses this "seat-of-the-pants" sense. Your journey through space in the mock-up space craft is filled with all the sights, sounds and vibrations you would expect. But the best illusion occurs when the booster rockets fire to separate stages. At the same time that you see and hear the rockets' blast, the seat cushion on which you are sitting (which you always thought was hard plastic) rapidly deflates. But it feels exactly as if the spaceship were shooting forward at some crazy speed and that you were being pushed down into the cushion. In the meantime, you never left the ground.

The balance sense is very different from the other senses. We do not "feel" its location. For example, we feel that our eyes see, our noses smell, our ears hear, and our skin touches. But where do we *feel* balance? If we are dizzy or seasick we feel sick to the stomach, we sweat, and our eyes might spin, but in no way do we feel anything we could call balance coming from the skull behind the ears—where the actual organs of balance are. These organs are housed in cavities in your skull right behind each ear canal. The balance sense is really two very different senses. Each one is simply built, and by looking at their design you can understand the way they work. Each is constructed differently and they do two very different jobs.

Yes, You Have Rocks in Your Head

One of the two balance organs is called the utricle (YOU-trih-cull). It was designed to do one very simple thing—detect if the head is tilted and by how much. This drawing shows the main parts of the utricle and you may already have some idea how it works. The actual sense cells are hair cells that signal one way if bent in one direction and signal another way when bent in the opposite direction. At one end they are attached to the skull. The other end sticks into a slab of jelly. The jelly is filled with heavy otoliths, which really means "ear stones." (So from now on, if someone asks "Do you have rocks in your head?" say "Why of course I do, so do YOU!")

Imagine what happens when you tilt your head backward.

The heavy slab slides backward a bit and bends the hair cells backward. The brain picks up these signals and figures out that the head is tilted backward. What could be simpler? This is the organ the brain uses to keep you from falling over.

Under normal, everyday conditions, this organ does its job perfectly without you even knowing it. But it can be fooled. The problem is that the utricle was designed for running and walking speeds and not for some of the wild things we now do in the

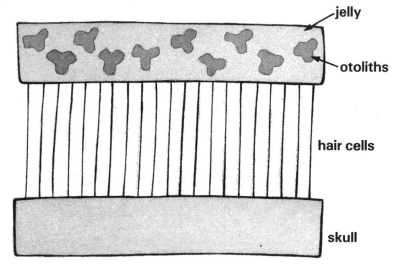

**The Utricle (Tilt-O-Meter)
when your head is untilted**

jelly

otoliths

hair cells

skull

twentieth century. For instance, spinning rides at amusement parks can produce a balance illusion. There is one ride in which people stand belted to the inside edge of a large cylinder, facing its centre. As it spins faster and faster around its centre, you feel the rotation, but you also feel as if your whole body is tilting backward more and more. This is pure illusion.

You know how water stays in a pail when you spin it around you? The same thing is happening in your utricle in this ride. The fast spinning forces your otoliths backward and your brain thinks you are tilting.

This same illusion can be extremely dangerous. Pilots of military jets speed up and slow down by huge amounts. For example, a jet taking off from an aircraft carrier is catapulted from 0 to 140 knots (0 to 250 km/hour) in just over three seconds. Can you imagine how much the pilot's hair cells are being bent backward? He may think he is climbing more than he should be, and dive into the ocean. Fortunately, he is trained to ignore that illusion, and to rely on his instruments, which are not being fooled.

head tilted back

hair cells are bent backwards

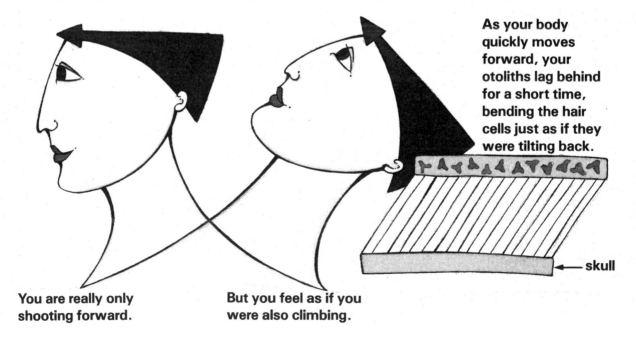

You are really only shooting forward.

But you feel as if you were also climbing.

As your body quickly moves forward, your otoliths lag behind for a short time, bending the hair cells just as if they were tilting back.

skull

Your Head, Like Venice, Has Canals

The other balance organ is not concerned with gravity, but is designed to tell the brain how you are moving. In fact, its only job is to tell the brain if you are rotating. You can rotate your head (and your body) in three ways: up-to-down (as when nodding YES); left-to-right (as when shaking your head to say NO); and clockwise to counterclockwise (tilt head over left then right shoulder). These are the three dimensions of space (3D). We have an organ that senses rotation in each one of those dimensions as this diagram shows. In fact we have a pair of these, one behind each ear.

Each one is known as a semicircular canal. Let's call it

Semicircular Canal

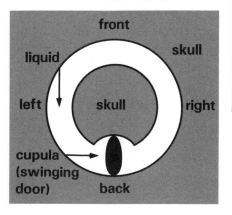

front
skull
liquid
left skull right
cupula (swinging door)
back

GUESS What?

Unlike science-fiction movies, we cannot yet remove gravity anywhere on Earth. But there are a few ways that astronauts can train here in preparation for the no-gravity (zero-g) of space. In one method, which is good for preparing for space walks outside the spacecraft, the trainee is fully suited-up and plunged into a deep pool. With the right weights and floats, that astronaut experiences close to zero-g. But what about training for inside the cabin? This next technique is ingenious. Using a hollowed-out and padded cargo jet, after reaching a certain speed the pilot flies a huge arc, smoothly up, then down (the shape is called a parabola). Around the top of the arc everyone in the plane

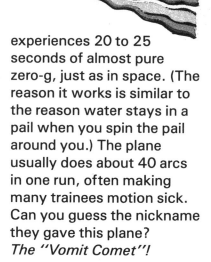

experiences 20 to 25 seconds of almost pure zero-g, just as in space. (The reason it works is similar to the reason water stays in a pail when you spin the pail around you.) The plane usually does about 40 arcs in one run, often making many trainees motion sick. Can you guess the nickname they gave this plane? *The "Vomit Comet"!*

SCC for short. As the name says, it is a hollowed tunnel in the skull that loops in a circle like the one in this diagram.

This one is a horizontal one; that is, if you place this page flat on a table, that is how the horizontal ones in your head

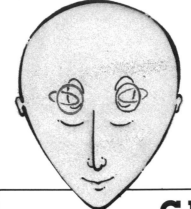

would be lying when you look straight ahead.

The other two pairs look the same but are in different positions. The SCC is filled with liquid. At some point the canal widens, and in that chamber is the actual sense organ called the cupula (Q-pew-lah). The cupula is attached to the skull on the outside of the canal and reaches across the chamber to the other side but is not attached there. It completely

head turns to the left

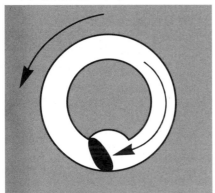

liquid pushes cupula to left

seals the chamber. The cupula acts as a swinging door. If the liquid pushes to the left, the door swings to the left. The cupula is packed with hair cells that send one kind of signal to the brain if they are bent in one direction, and another signal when bent in the opposite direction. So, the hair cells and the brain can tell which way the cupula

swings. Notice that this organ was not designed to detect gravity. Except under very special conditions, the cupula will never move no matter what *position* your head is in because it does not float or sink in the liquid.

GUESS What?

Some people are silly enough to drink so much alcohol that they get dizzy. You can figure out why. The cupula has many blood vessels, the SCC has very few. So the alcohol in the blood is absorbed very quickly by the cupula and extremely slowly by the surrounding liquid. Alcohol is lighter than water (which is the main ingredient in the liquid in the SCCs). That means all the cupulas are floating in their SCCs and signalling to the brain that the drunk must be spinning. This is one time that the SCCs are influenced by gravity. But, of course, we weren't designed with alcohol in mind.

LET'S DO it!

One basic rule in nature is that things are lazy. Scientists call this laziness "inertia." It simply means that things want to stay the way they are. Things that are standing still want to stay standing still. Things that are moving want to keep on moving. Check it out yourself.

What You Need

a deep bowl
water
dry rice, or peas, or beans

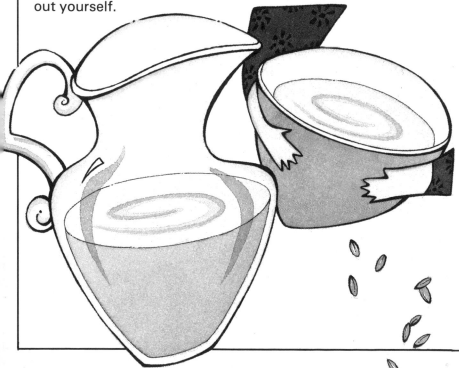

What To Do

Half fill the bowl with water and sprinkle a few grains of rice into it (so you can easily see the water move.) Grasp the bowl on opposite sides and give it a quick half-turn. The water did not turn. (Keep that bowl of water, you will need it again.) This is exactly what happens inside your horizontal SCC when you turn your head. When you turn your head to the left, the liquid stays still and pushes your cupula to the left, and that is the signal sent to the brain. Simple, isn't it? You can figure out for yourself how you have to move your head to make the other SCCs work.

LET'S DO it Again!

Dizziness is the feeling of spinning while you are standing perfectly still. Why do you get dizzy after spinning for a long time, and why do your eyes jerk left and right? Now that you know how SCCs work, the answer is really quite simple. But first let's experiment.

What You Need

several friends
a blindfold
wide open flat field or lawn of short, soft grass with no obstacles

What To Do

1 Blindfold one friend and slowly spin her around ten times to the left.

2 Quickly stop the friend, remove the blindfold, and ask her to walk forward in a perfectly straight line.

3 Repeat step 1 with another friend.

4 Quickly stop him, remove the blindfold, and watch his eyes.

During step 2, your friend probably started to walk (or fall) to the left. During step 4, you probably saw his eyes jerk to the right. The answer involves inertia again, so get out your bowl of water and rice. This time, place the bowl on the centre of something that spins: a swivel chair; a spinning serving platter; a record player (ask permission); or take it outside to one of those merry-go-rounds in playgrounds. Slowly but steadily spin the bowl around its centre. At first the water stands still, but then it slowly catches up with the bowl. Abruptly stop the bowl. The water will keep spinning for some time. This is exactly what happens inside your SCCs, as these diagrams show.

head spins steadily to the left

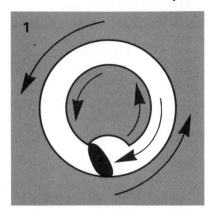

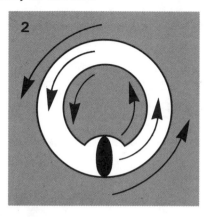

head stops

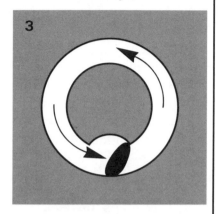

At first "lazy" liquid pushes cupula to left.

Soon, liquid catches up with skull and cupula is unbent.

Liquid still flushing in old direction pushes cupula to right.

This is what happens inside your horizontal SCC while you steadily spin around to the left, and then stop.

- You already understand Stage #1, except that another thing happens here. Your eyes jerk left and right because your brain is trying to catch up with the blurry, spinning world. This is a reflex.
- In Stage #2, the liquid has caught up with the SCC so the cupula returns to its normal position. [Notice that this means that it would not be signalling. In fact, if you could spin with your eyes closed and your body perfectly still on a noiseless merry-go-round, you would not feel as

though you were spinning at all during this stage. Normally, we feel rotation from other senses, such as vision and touch.]

- After you have stopped (Stage #3), the liquid still rushes around for a while, pushing the cupula in the other direction. So, even though you have stopped, your brain now thinks you are spinning in the opposite direction, and that is the feeling of dizziness. Your eyes jerk because, again, the brain is trying to catch up with the world it incorrectly thinks is spinning.

Soon the liquid slows down and all is back to normal

(unless the spinning started motion sickness!). You may have noticed that during dizziness, if you spin in the opposite direction the dizzy spell is shortened. You should now be able to figure out why. (*Hint:* Look at Stage #3 and imagine spinning in the other direction.)

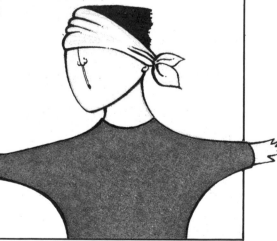

GUESS What?

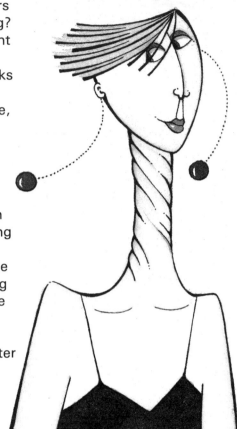

Why do dancers and skaters not feel dizzy after spinning? This is actually two different questions. Dancers spot. That means the dancer looks at something (spots), such as someone in the audience, and holds the head there while the body turns, then quickly snaps the head around back to that spot. During the rapid snaps the liquid cannot catch up with the SCC, and when spinning stops, the liquid is not spinning either. You can see this for yourself by spinning your bowl of water and rice in short, fast jerks with longer pauses between. If you do it just right, the water never spins.

Figure skaters spin too fast to spot—nine to ten rounds per second. If they spotted at those speeds, they might break their necks! It seems that skaters have learned to ignore signals that come from the SCCs after a spin, and instead, rely on the vision, touch, and body senses, which are telling the brain correctly that everything is stable. Skaters who have not practised for a while are usually extremely dizzy after spins and have to relearn this. This learning is so complete that they even suppress the jerky eye movements after a spin. This is interesting because reflexes are usually very hard or impossible to control—but these guys somehow do it!

Animal Magnetism

What would happen if your Otoliths were made of iron? If a strong magnet were held behind your head, you would feel like you were tilting backwards (and your reflexes might tell you to dive onto your face!). This idea has been tested in some types of crayfish, which have a somewhat differently designed balance sense. They have a small cavity lined all around with touch cells filled with water and a grain of sand. The place the grain settles indicates where down is. Scientists have harmlessly fooled this system by replacing the sand in the aquarium with iron filings. (When the crayfish moults {sheds its skin}, it also replaces the sand, but now it will take in a filing.) They held a strong magnet over the crayfish's carapace (the solid part of its back), and the crayfish tried very hard to roll over onto its back, because the filing was now touching the top of the chamber which normally signals down! This experiment was perfectly harmless, since the animal was later allowed to replace the iron with normal sand.

DID YOU EVER
Wonder?

If you have ever experienced motion sickness, you know exactly how horrible that ''barfy'' feeling is. For some people, a playground swing is enough to start it. For others, a car or boat ride will bring it on. Apparently a camel ride is the ''best'' for producing strong motion sickness in the largest number of people. Scientists are still working on why we experience motion sickness. The simple theory is that there is a ''mismatch'' between the visual, touch and balance senses. Your inner ear is signalling rocking back and forth while your ship's cabin looks perfectly still and level (supposedly, that's why looking out a porthole at the horizon sometimes helps to calm the stomach). But the REAL question is still unanswered: why should a mismatch cause you to vomit? It makes total sense to have a reflex that will make you barf after you have been poisoned—by getting the poison out of your stomach your life may be saved! But

why after a camel ride? Dr. Ken Money, of DCIEM Canada, thinks that this ''mismatch'' is actually similar to what happens to your senses during poisoning; a camel ride accidentally trips the vomiting reflex (his full theory is way too complicated for this book). He is also studying why astronauts get sick in space. This is a very serious problem. Imagine, it costs many millions of dollars to keep each astronaut up there, and almost three-quarters of them will experience some motion sickness and almost one-quarter will be so sick that they cannot work! That is expensive! One of Dr. Money's biggest problems is finding a test on earth that will predict who will vomit in space. Canadian astronaut Dr. Roberta Bondar performed several of Dr. Money's studies on the Discovery Space Shuttle mission in January 1992. Dr. Money was her back-up.

Eye See!

Vision

Vision, the seeing sense, is the one humans use most. The part of the brain for vision is larger than the areas of all the other senses combined. Probably for these reasons, scientists know more about vision than any of the other senses.

Our eyes are like mobile, well-coordinated video cameras that send to the brain signals about patterns of light. The brain immediately

light—such as the sun or a lamp—or reflects light—such as the moon or this page. Light travels outward from the source or surface in all directions, and your eyes are made to let in the light. The cornea is the clear bump on the front outside of your eyes. Close your lids and gently feel your corneas as you roll your eyes around. The cornea gathers the spreading light to form an image (picture) of

The inside back of the eyeball is covered by 128 million sense cells, called rods (120 million) and cones (8 million), which change the light into signals that the brain understands. This layer is called the retina (REH-tih-nuh) and contains many more cells that connect the sense cells together and to the brain. The centre of the retina—the part of your eye you use when you look **AT** something—is called the fovea

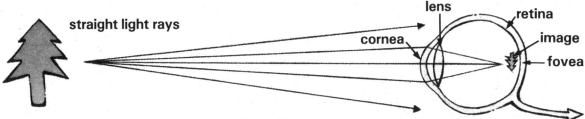

straight light rays
lens
retina
cornea
image
fovea
optic nerve signals to brain

organizes these signals to produce what we call vision.

The seeing sense starts with light. Just about everything in the universe either gives off

whatever you are looking at on the back inside of your eyeball. The lens fine-tunes the image to bring it into exact focus on the retina.

(FOE-vee-ah). All the rest is called the periphery (purr-RIH-fur-ree). The brain organizes and analyzes these signals and produces sight.

GUESS
What?

You probably know about people who are short-sighted or long-sighted. For them, the image is fuzzy because the cornea and lens do not focus the image **exactly** on the retina. But there is another problem which few of us know about, but which almost everyone has, called "astigmatism" (as-TIG-muh-tizm). In most of us, the astigmatism is mild and isn't easily noticed in everyday seeing. But this star figure might bring it out. Look around its centre, and carefully notice if some lines seem blurrier than others. Usually the vertical or horizontal lines are fuzzy, and not the tilted ones. If you wear glasses, take them off and see! How can you prove to yourself that the blur is in your eye and not on the page? (*Hint:* Rotate the star pattern.)

DID YOU EVER
Wonder?

You probably know that you have a blind spot in each eye. You are blind in that spot because there are about one million nerves heading out to the optic nerve to the brain and there is just no room for rods and cones. The real question is: Why aren't there two "black holes" in the world right now? It seems that the brain fills in those holes with different patterns. For fun, make your own blind spot demo, but put one pattern under the left half of the dot and a different one under the right half. See which pattern your brain chooses to fill in. Also try differently coloured halves.

These kinds of "holes" in your field of vision are normal. But many people also suffer from abnormal on the optic nerves and cause blindness in half the visual field of each eye similar to, but worse than, a horse's blinders. Goliath probably couldn't have seen people or objects coming from either side. The battle was unfair alright. Goliath never knew what hit him (or where it came from)! The amazing thing about these people is that most are

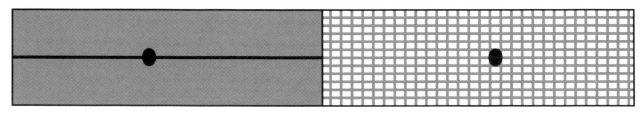

whatever is around the edges of the holes. See for yourself. To find the blind spot in your right eye, close the left and look only at the left dot. Starting with the page 10 cm from your nose, slowly move the page away from you until the right dot disappears (while you are looking at the left dot). Do not move the page and look at the right dot with only your left eye. You found your blind spots. But notice that there were no holes. Rather, they were filled in by the holes which can take up large areas. Some, for instance, cannot see anything to the left of where they are looking in either eye. Others cannot see in the left field of the left eye and the right of the right eye. This may explain the well-known Biblical tale of how little David, against overwhelming odds, slew the mighty giant Goliath. A vision scientist speculates that Goliath had a type of tumour in the brain which often causes giantism. This tumour can also press

totally unaware that the large hole exists. Some simply ignore it—*there really are men* who shave only the half of the face they can see—this is called Visual Neglect. Others move their eyes around to use the part of the retina which can see.

Two Retinas?

Rods differ from cones in many ways that directly affect the way we see. In fact, most scientists think we actually have two retinas blended into one. Here are just a few differences:

	Rods	Cones
Location	Periphery	Fovea
Light Level	Nighttime	Daytime
"See" Colour?	No	Yes
Types	1	3

Let's explore some of these differences. Acuity is a measure of the smallest size you can see. Your fovea has the best acuity—it can see the tiniest detail. As you move out from the fovea into the periphery, your acuity becomes worse and worse. See for yourself by looking directly at your fingertip (you are using your fovea). You should be able to see the tiny grooves of your fingerprints. Now keep looking forward, but swing your hand out to the side where you can just barely see it (in the extreme periphery). You probably cannot even count the number of fingers!

GUESS What?

Some nocturnal creatures such as mice, rats and bats have mostly, or only, rods in their retinas. They have great difficulty telling colours apart and are almost blind in full sunlight, but are perfectly suited to seeing at night. Other creatures, such as pigeons, chickens, turtles and most reptiles have only cones in their retinas. They have no trouble distinguishing colours and see perfectly well during the day, but are totally blind at night.

LET'S DO it!

White light, like that from the sun, is a mixture of all the colours of the rainbow. When the brain receives such a signal, it decides "WHITE." A sweater that we call blue, for instance, is not blue by itself. Rather, it absorbs all the other coloured light rays and reflects only the blue rays into the eye.

There are three types of cones: those sensitive to blue light, others to green light, and still others to red light. Only the "blue" cones are excited by blue light, and that is the signal that is sent to the brain. "Green" cones detect the green light rays coming from grass and "red" cones are excited by the red rays reflected off tomatoes. There is something odd about the "blue" cones. "Red" and "green" cones are densely packed in the fovea, but blue cones are sprinkled only here and there, and in the very, very centre there are no "blue" cones. Try this experiment and see.

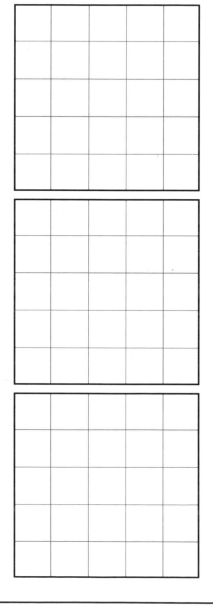

What You Need

three felt markers or pencil crayons or paints: one pure blue, one pure green, and one pure red (find markers or pencils that produce colours of the same brightness)
light photocopies or tracings of these checkerboards, so that the grey lines are barely visible
tape

What To Do

1 Colour each checkerboard. Make one red and white, one green and white, and one blue and white.

2 Tape the sheet to an outside wall where you can easily and safely walk back from it.

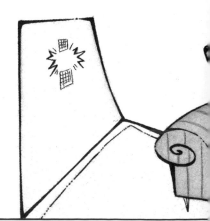

3 Walk back and closely observe which checkerboard disappears first.

If all went well, the blue checkerboard disappeared first, and you might have had to walk twice as far away to make the red or green checkerboards disappear. By walking backwards, you made the checkerboards smaller on your retina. Since the blue checkerboard disappeared first, the acuity of your blue system must be worse than the green or red system. In other words, at the place on the retina where our acuity is the absolute best, there are no blue cones (only red and green ones) and we are blue-blind!

(If your experiment did not work, can you figure out why? *Hint:* Were the colours equally bright?)

GUESS
What?

Many years ago a poet once said, "The eyes are the windows to the soul." He did not know how right he was! As a baby develops in the womb, the eyes do grow out of the brain (the seat of the soul?). When you talk with someone you usually watch the eyes, probably because they show the emotions. People who do not keep eye contact are thought to be hiding something. And your pupil— the black hole in the

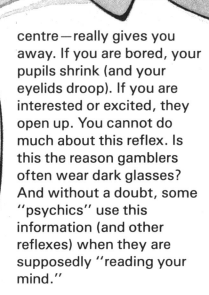

centre—really gives you away. If you are bored, your pupils shrink (and your eyelids droop). If you are interested or excited, they open up. You cannot do much about this reflex. Is this the reason gamblers often wear dark glasses? And without a doubt, some "psychics" use this information (and other reflexes) when they are supposedly "reading your mind."

In a Flash

Most of us have had the experience of looking directly into the flash of a camera. Afterwards, we are temporarily blinded in a spot that is the same size and in the same place as the original flash. This is called an afterimage. Your rods and cones in that part of the retina were temporarily "bleached" by the strong light, which makes them very insensitive.

As the rods and cones slowly became "unbleached," seeing returned to normal. By the way, this is the same reason you have difficulty seeing in a dark movie theatre after walking in from the bright outdoors. Outdoors, your whole retina was light adapted. In the theatre, most rods and cones were too bleached to work. But as you sat in the dark, the rods and cones slowly returned to

normal, and your vision improved. You became dark adapted. Just for fun, the next time you are just sitting around in bright sunshine, completely close and cover one eye for at least ten minutes, and look around with the other eye. Then uncover the eye and compare how the world looks through your light-adapted eye and your dark-adapted (covered) eye.

LET'S DO it!

Coloured afterimages are especially interesting because they follow very exact rules.

What You Need

several photocopies or traces of the Canadian flag outline
coloured markers, pencils, or paints

What To Do

1. Colour the maple leaf and the two bands on either side with strong, pure green.

2. Stare at the dot in the centre for at least one minute (try very hard not to look anywhere else).

3. Then quickly look at the dot of an uncoloured copy of the flag.

At first, the green Canadian flag looked very odd. But after adapting to it for one minute, the uncoloured flag looked like a pale, but correctly coloured flag. This tells us two things. First, separate cones do not send their single messages to the brain. Instead, messages are combined between cones. Second, not just any messages are combined. Adapting to green always produces a red afterimage, and adapting to red always produces a green

afterimage. Try it and see.

Somehow, green and red cones are connected in a balanced and opposite way. So, for example, if the green cones are bleached (by adapting to green paint, or from a green flash), the red/green pair is unbalanced, and the brain decides "red" until the green signal returns to normal as the green cones unbleach. Red and green are called opponent colours. Blue and yellow are also opponents. Try them on the flag.

Oh Canada?

Seeing What Is Not There

Rods also do not send their separate signals to the brain. In fact, they are even more connected to each other than most cones are. In this simple demonstration you will see something that is not really there.

Look at the grey bands that go from dark to light. Within each one of these bands the grey or black is the same all over. That is, the black in the left band is exactly the same from edge to edge. The grey in the neighbouring band is the same all over.

This shows a very basic rule of vision: Light areas make neighbouring dark areas look even darker, and dark areas make light areas look even lighter. Edges are the important things in the visual image. Our visual system looks for edges and makes them stand out even more. By the way, this edge effect happens in the retina as well as the brain. To prove to yourself that the steps are really flat, pick one band in the middle, and totally cover its two neighbours with two pieces of thick paper. The lips and dips

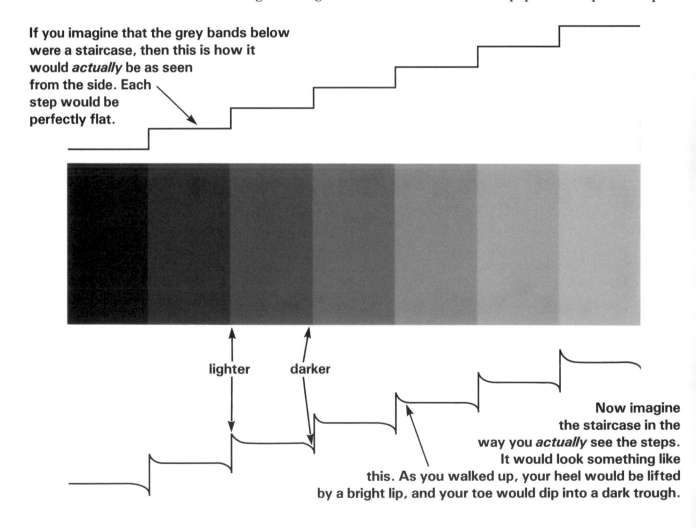

If you imagine that the grey bands below were a staircase, then this is how it would *actually* be as seen from the side. Each step would be perfectly flat.

lighter   darker

Now imagine the staircase in the way you *actually* see the steps. It would look something like this. As you walked up, your heel would be lifted by a bright lip, and your toe would dip into a dark trough.

should disappear.

Now look below to the "Jiggly Eyes" experiment. Pay attention to the intersections—the places where the white lines cross. You should see "ghost-like" grey spots: the intersections seem darker than the lines. You can figure out why. Remember the rule: Light areas make neighbouring dark areas look even darker, and dark areas make light areas look even lighter. The lines are surrounded by more dark than the intersections. So the lines appear brighter than the intersections. In the picture on the right, the ring is really the same greyness all around, but why does it not seem that way? (*Hint:* Remember the rule!)

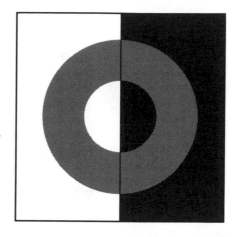

Jiggly Eyes

Look at the dot of this letter "i" and keep your eyes on it as steadily as you can. You probably think your eyes are perfectly motionless, but that could not be farther from the truth. Our eyes are constantly jiggling in their sockets, and there is nothing you can do about it.

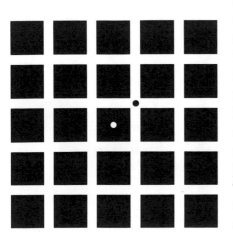

Normally you don't notice it, probably because the whole image on your retina and all the parts in it are moving together. But if you could compare the image to something that was not moving on the retina, you should see the motion.

When you stare at something bright or at an object for a long time, you will see an afterimage when you look away. An afterimage is an image that lasts long after the real image has gone. An interesting thing about afterimages is that they do not move. So, if your eye is jiggling, that afterimage is "glued" to the same part of the retina, but the real image is drifting and jiggling across it.

Stare at the white dot in the grid and count to 20 (to form an afterimage). Then stare at the black dot and count to 20. Keep doing this back and forth, and notice that no matter how still you think you are holding your eyes, the afterimage is never steady.

LET'S DO it!

The visual brain is filled with cells designed to detect lines and edges in the image. Some look for vertical lines, some for horizontal, and others for tilted lines. Some detectors are designed to see fat lines, others see skinny lines, and still others look for medium-sized lines. These cells are the beginning of the brain's organization of the signals coming from the retina. You can play with your tilt detectors and find out more about how the brain works. Read the instructions first, then do the experiment.

1 Convince yourself that the lines on the right are perfectly straight and vertical.

2 Look anywhere inside the rectangle between the tilted lines for one minute. Make sure you look around in that space and not just at one point. (We do not want an afterimage.)

3 Now quickly look at the X between the straight lines. Are the straight lines now tilted the opposite way? What happened here?

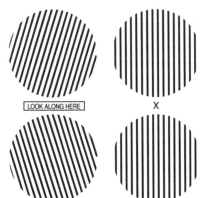

LOOK ALONG HERE

X

A Chorus in the Brain

When a detector sees its favourite type of line it becomes excited, and signals rapidly (as if it screamed loudly). When you look at perfectly vertical lines, for example, your vertical detectors signal the most, but the ones that detect lines tilted just a little to the left and the ones that detect lines tilted a little to the right also signal a little bit. Of course, the horizontal detectors do not signal at all.

The lines appear vertical because the vertical detectors signal the most. When you look at lines tilted slightly to the right, the right detectors now signal the most, the vertical detectors signal a little less, and the left detectors do not signal at all. So, for now, you see lines tilting to the right. But if you continue to look at the lines tilting to the right, the right detectors become tired and cannot signal at all (the vertical detectors are also very weak). But the left detectors are not tired at all, so when you now look at vertical lines, they appear tilted to the left because the left detectors are screaming the loudest. Soon all the detectors get their strength back, and all is normal again.

What You See Depends on Your Point of View

What is this figure on the left? Why, a square of course! And the figure beside it is obviously a diamond! This is

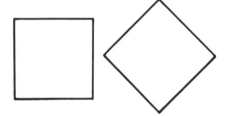

interesting because the only difference between a square and a diamond is that one has been rotated. In other words, what you see depends on your point of view. If that is so, then turn your head clockwise and judge the two shapes. The diamond still looks like a diamond, and the square, a square. ˎ

Notice what this must mean. You are *not* judging from the way the figure sits on your retina, but from the way it is oriented in the outside world! In other words, you are using gravity—vision is being influenced by your balance sense (and visual cues about gravity). A few artists have known about this and have

created figures that "toy" with our visual systems. This illustration is one our artist adapted from Rex Whistler, who created many figures like this. Tilt your head just a little bit clockwise, then the other way. Notice that when you have one face, the other face is difficult, or impossible to see.

Are Two Eyes Better Than One?

Why do we have two eyes pointing forward when most creatures have eyes on the side of the head and have a very wide, panoramic view of the

world? What did our "designer" trade for panoramic vision? We gained stereo-vision.

Each of our eyes has a slightly different view of the

same world. Check it out for yourself. Line up your two fingers to the right eye as shown in this picture. Now close your right eye, open the left and see how the fingers

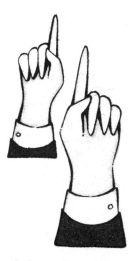

left eye's view

right eye's view

shows you how to use a mirror so that the left half goes to the left eye, and the right half goes to the right eye. (This stereogram is really the same as the picture at left except the right half has been flipped left-right because the right eye will see it through a mirror, which flips it back again.) If you position your head carefully and look through the mirror at the diagram with only the right eye (the left eye looks straight at its half on paper), the big finger should seem to "pop-out" and really look as though it is in front. That is stereovision.

The next stereogram is of the interesting art of Kim Fernandes who creates 3D

are now separated. Open both eyes and notice how you see only one picture and the fingers are in depth—3D! Your brain combined the two slightly different images into one and pulled out the third dimension, depth. If we could

show the left view to the left eye only, and the right view to the right eye only we should be able to recreate the depth effect.

This pair of pictures below (fingers) is called a stereogram. The diagram on the next page

Illustration: Kim Fernandes

pictures from modelling clay. About 8 in 100 people cannot see depth in stereograms— they are stereoblind.

You can draw stereograms by hand, or if you have access to a computer with fairly good graphics, stereograms are also easy to make that way. One important step is to make a good, easily seen frame (it does not have to be a rectangle like those here). Make one-half the stereogram, duplicate it, and slide it to one side (move it left-to-right only, not up-down). You now have two identical pictures horizontally aligned. Can you guess what would happen if you viewed these together? That's right, they would be perfectly flat. You have to move some elements of

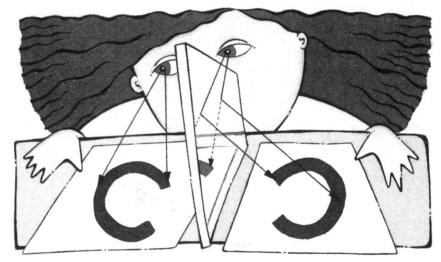

your graphic in only one of the two halves *slightly* to the left or right. Then just flip left-to-right (make a mirror image) of the half that will be viewed through the mirror. You can view it directly on the computer's monitor with the mirror, and quickly learn the

effects of different changes. Once you have some good ones, print them out to show your friends. Scans of people's faces are a lot of fun to play around with (making noses or lips stick *way* out, for example).

NOW Hear This!

Hearing

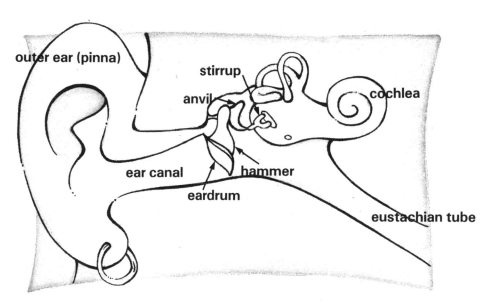

outer ear (pinna)

stirrup

anvil

cochlea

ear canal

hammer

eardrum

eustachian tube

Stop everything you are doing and listen. Listen to all the different kinds of sounds that you probably did not notice while you were reading. You might hear the harsh sounds of traffic or construction, the peaceful sounds of birds, music, or moving water, or just the sound of someone speaking— the most complicated sound of all. Why can you hear them and how do you know what they are? The answers to these questions lie in a system of tubes and tunnels inside your head.

The sense of hearing begins with the ear and ends in the brain. Those funny looking, curled-up things on the sides of your head (called pinnas) that hold your glasses up are only a small part of what makes hearing possible.

That hole in your outer ear is the ear canal, which contains the eardrum. It stretches tightly across the whole canal and vibrates when air waves push it.

The inside of the eardrum is attached to the three smallest bones in your body, the hammer, anvil and stirrup. These bones vibrate with the eardrum and send those vibrations to a covered window, which is the entrance to the next part called the cochlea (COKE-lee-ah), or inner ear. The cochlea is a snail-shaped tunnel in your skull that contains the cells

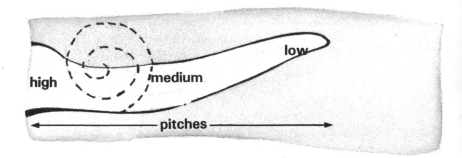

high · medium · low

pitches

that communicate to the brain. It would be easier to figure out if we could uncurl it and lay it out flat as in this diagram (of course that cannot actually be done). The cochlea is filled with liquid and a long thin tissue runs along the full length, dividing the liquid in half. That tissue, called the basilar membrane (BAH-zih-lar), is the secret to how hearing works.

The basilar membrane holds a little more than 15,000 hair cells. When the hair cells are bent, they signal to the brain. Cells in the stirrup end of the membrane signal high-pitched sounds, and the ones at the opposite end signal low pitches. The whole range is ordered nicely along the length. The basilar membrane moves in waves when the liquid is vibrating. High pitches cause waves at the stirrup end, and low pitches produce the biggest wave at the opposite end. The brain "listens" to which hair cells are signalling the most and decides which pitch that sound is. By the way, there are absolutely no blood vessels near the cochlea. Can you imagine the deafening sound that would be produced by tidal waves in the liquid caused by your pulse?

GUESS What?

Listening to very loud sounds, especially for a long time, can cause serious and permanent hearing loss. These kinds of sounds produce abnormally huge waves in the basilar membrane, which tear the hair cells apart. Hair cells cannot replace themselves. That is why loud sounds should be avoided at all times—like loud music, aircraft, heavy machinery, and even loud vacuum cleaners. Scientists recently discovered that many pig farmers suffer a severe and permanent hearing loss. And those that have tended pigs the longest have the greatest loss. That is because at feeding time pigs squeal for joy. About 1000 pigs can produce a squeal almost as loud as a clap of very loud thunder right above your head!

DID YOU EVER
Wonder?

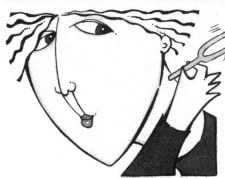

Why does your voice on a recording sound so different from your normal voice? Sound waves can get to your inner ear in two ways. You know the standard way: through the air, eardrum, hammer, anvil, stirrup, and to the cochlea. The other way is through the bone around the cochlea. When you speak, your vocal cords shake the air *and* your skull, and you hear both. The recording of your voice is only taken through the standard air path. You can check out the bone path by striking a tuning fork and firmly touching its base to the bony bump just behind your ear (that is as close to the cochlea as you can get). The tuning fork shakes your skull, which shakes your cochlea. If someone has a hearing loss, the doctor checks out both paths. If the loss is there with the bone path, nothing can be done because there is nerve damage. But if the loss is only in the air path, it means your inner ear is just fine. The problem lies in your eardrum or the three bones. These problems can often be fixed.

What Do You Hear?

Stop again and listen. Can you explain what is making the sounds that you hear? All the sounds are caused by something. In other words, all sounds have a source.

All sources of sound vibrate, or shake back and forth. These vibrations move through the air to your ear, and your brain tells you what the vibrations mean.

For example, if your cat meows, she is the source of the vibrations making the sound. You know the sound is a meow and not a dog's bark because the vibrations are different and your brain has learned the difference.

Sound sources can vibrate fast or slowly. A tuning fork is a good example. This diagram shows how the prongs of the tuning fork move back and forth. But the way the prongs move can change.

The speed of vibration can change. We hear fast

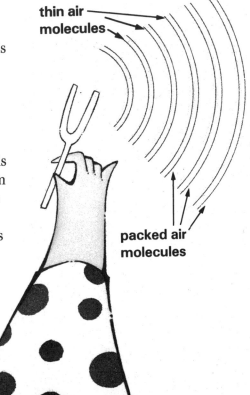

thin air molecules

packed air molecules

73

vibrations as having a high pitch, such as the sound from a piccolo. Slow vibrations have a low pitch, such as the sound a bassoon makes. And there is a huge range between. The speed of vibration is called frequency (FREE-kwen-see): how fast the prongs move back and forth.

The prongs can also change in the amount they vibrate, or how *far* they move back and forth. If they move a little, the sound is quiet (if there is no movement, there is no sound). If they move back and forth a huge amount, the sound is loud. This amount of movement is called amplitude

(AM-plih-tewd). Frequency and amplitude can be changed separately. In other words, a piccolo can sound loud or quiet, and so can a bassoon.

Air is usually in the space between the sound source and our ears. But sound energy can also travel through water or metal.

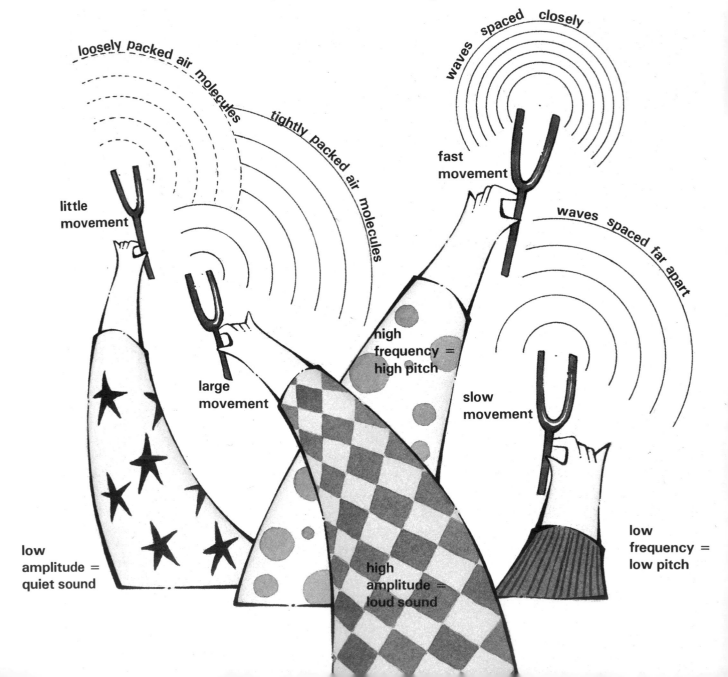

Air is a gas made up of loosely spaced molecules. The air carries the energy from the source to your ears. The tuning fork, as it moves forward, pushes the air molecules closely together. As it moves back, the air molecules loosen up. The sound travels outward from the source in growing waves, just like the waves from a stone you drop into a pond. The wave is similar to the wave carried by a row of tumbling dominoes or the spectators at a baseball game.

The same thing happens with other sound sources, a vibrating bassoon reed, piano, violin or guitar string, your own vocal chords, a loudspeaker, or jackhammer. Large motions produce very densely packed molecules; small motions produce loosely packed molecules. Fast motions produce closely packed waves; slow motions produce waves that are spaced out.

You can play around with frequency and amplitude by stretching an elastic band around an open box, like the bottom of a shoe box. Pluck the elastic gently and strongly, and pluck it while stretching the elastic different amounts. Listen to the differences.

DID YOU EVER Wonder?

When a race car, motorcycle, or locomotive zooms by you, have you ever wondered why its pitch is first high as it travels toward you, and then drops to a lower pitch the moment it passes you—even though you know that the motor is running at the exact same speed all the time? This shift in pitch is called the Doppler Shift—being named after the scientist Christian Doppler who figured it out in the last century. When the race car, for instance, is standing still with the motor running (fast or slow), all the sound waves are growing out from the engine evenly spaced, no matter where you stand. But when the car begins to move, the waves bunch up in front of the car, and become spaced out behind the car. So, the frequency of waves in front of the car really is higher than behind the car. As the car passes you, you first get the high frequencies, then the low frequencies from behind, and you hear the "screeeeeeoooooooom." Notice that for the driver, the sound is a steady pitch, because his ears are always the same distance from the motor.

standing still

same frequency all around

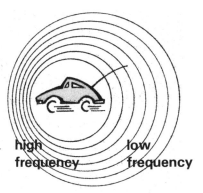

racing to the left

high frequency   low frequency

LET'S DO it!

See Hear!

You can build a simple gadget that will let you "see" sound waves.

What You Need

a friend
a can with both ends removed
balloon with the neck cut off
small piece of mirror about 2 cm by 2 cm or smaller (your local hardware store can give you some scrap pieces free)
glue or double-sided tape
elastic bands
strong flashlight

What To Do

1 Stretch the balloon tightly over one end of the can like a drum, and wrap the elastic band around to hold it there.

2 Glue the mirror on the outside of the balloon about halfway between the edge and the centre.

3 Place the can on its side on a table top with the mirror facing a light-coloured wall 1 to 2 metres away.

4 Darken the room and have your friend point the flashlight at the mirror as shown. Look for the reflection of light on the wall.

5 Hold the can firmly so it does not move (two plasticine "fingers" on either side of the can would work well), and scream into the open end of the can. Try different pitches.

6 Watch the spot of light vibrate.

The sound waves from your vibrating vocal chords vibrated the balloon. The tightly packed molecules of air pushed the balloon outward, and the loosely packed ones pulled it back. If you changed the pitch of your screams enough, the light spot should have vibrated more quickly with the high pitch than with the low pitch. If it didn't, place a loudspeaker behind your gadget, and play some music with a heavy beat (rock music or the 1812 Overture by Tchaikovsky—it has real cannon blasts). Watch how the spot jiggles rapidly with the high notes and more slowly with lower notes, and does huge jumps with thumps or cannon blasts. Notice that this balloon vibrates just as your eardrum does.

GUESS
What?

If you have ever flown with a commercial airline, you know that just before takeoff and landing the flight attendants hand out candies. While this is a nice touch, they do not do this just to make the skies friendly. Your middle ear is filled with air. For the eardrum to work at its best, the pressure in the middle ear has to be identical to the outside air pressure. That is why you have a Eustachian tube (you-STAY-shun) that connects the middle ear to your throat. The air in your throat is the same as outside air. As the plane is taking off or landing, the pressure in the plane's cabin becomes lower or higher than pressure on the ground you left behind, and that difference can push the eardrum painfully. Some people automatically equalize the pressure, sometimes by yawning. Swallowing also helps, and that is what the candies are for, to get you to swallow. Often you hear little babies crying at these times. That is because they do not know they should swallow. People with colds or throat infections also often feel ear pain, because their swollen throats have closed the tube. By the way, the tube gets its wonderful name from Bartolommeo Eustachio; the Italian doctor who discovered it in the 1500s.

LET'S DO it!

Some sounds normally are too faint to hear. One of these is your friend's heartbeat, even with your ear right up against the chest. You can make a simple gadget that will amplify (make louder) that sound.

What You Need & What To Do

- Snugly fit the small end of a large funnel into a hose or tube 0.5 to 1 metre long.
- Hold the open end of the funnel against your friend's chest, just to the left (about 5 to 10 cm) of the hard breastbone in the centre.
- Hold the other end close to your ear and listen to the heartbeat (and to other sounds).

The faint sound waves from your heart spread out in all directions. So, normally, only a few of them reach your ear. The funnel gathered all the sound waves coming from the heart and concentrated them down the tube to your ear.

Can you guess what you have just reinvented? That's right—a stethoscope—originally invented in 1819 by the French doctor, René-Théophile-Hyacynthe Laënnec, to listen in on all the beats, gasps and gurgles inside you.

By the way, your stethoscope can also amplify sounds the other way around. Purse your lips and blow a raspberry—the kind of sound a trumpet player makes—into the tube end of your stethoscope. Notice how much louder this sound is now, than without the stethoscope. Keep this gadget. You will need it later as part of another experiment.

Why Do We Have Two Ears?

Imagine being in the jungle on a pitch-black night. You know that there are hungry tigers in the area and you have to be on the alert. Since your eyes cannot help you, you have to rely on your other senses. Imagine you heard a very long roar. One ear would be just fine if all you wanted to know was the direction of the tiger's roar. Just turn your head left to right and stop where the sound is the loudest.

There are two serious limits to this technique. First, it tells you only the direction of the source, not *how far* it is. Is it a loud tiger miles away, or a hungry tiger with laryngitis within pouncing distance?

Second, what if the tiger did not roar, but instead, just stepped on a nearby twig and produced a very short snap. There is no time to zero-in with only one ear. In the chapter on vision you discovered that we have two eyes so we can see accurately in depth. Guess what—we have two ears so that we can *hear* accurately in depth. One ear gives us a crude idea of the direction something is. Two ears tell us where and give an idea of how far.

The way the brain does all this is quite simple. Look at loudspeaker A in the diagram. It is straight ahead. Both ears hear its sound at exactly the same time and with exactly the same loudness. Now look at loudspeaker B. Its sound is louder and earlier to the left ear than to the right. You can imagine the results of many other locations. The brain listens for loudness and time differences between the ears, and quickly calculates where the sound source must be. Notice also that A and B could never be confused.

This is crudely how the system works, but there must be more to it. Take a look at loudspeaker C. It is the mirror image of B. It produces the same loudness and time differences between the ears that loudspeaker B did. And yet we can easily tell them apart. In the next experiment you will learn another cue that your hearing sense uses to locate confusing sounds.

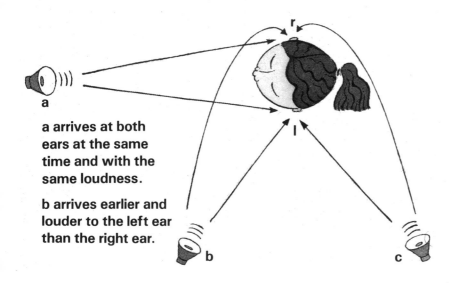

a arrives at both ears at the same time and with the same loudness.

b arrives earlier and louder to the left ear than the right ear.

79

LET'S DO it!

In this experiment you will discover why your pinna has such funny squiggly curves.

What You Need

large earmuffs, or a wide winter headband, or the old-fashioned headphones that fully cover both ears
a good blindfold
several friends

What To Do

1. In a fairly large room, have a friend (subject) kneel in the most open space.

2. Blindfold the subject.

3. One person will then snap the fingers at many different locations around the subject. Stay more than an arm's length away.

Also, move silently so the only cue the subject has is the snap, not your feet shuffling. The subject's job is to point to the snap.

4. Concentrate your snaps along the subject's midline (see diagram), and see how well he or she can point.

5. Once the subject is well trained, keep the blindfold on, and cover the ears with the earmuffs, headband, or headphones. Make sure both pinnas are fully covered.

6. Repeat steps 3 and 4.

First, with only the blindfold, the subject should have become quite good at pointing. In other words, just as with many of the other senses, we also have a "hearing map" of the world

around us. (A bit of training was needed because we rely much more on vision and we do not use this map often, but the map is there.) If the outer ears were completely covered, pointing probably became more sloppy, because the folds and ridges in your outer ears help to locate sounds. Notice also that your outer ears "point" forward a bit.

Before the sound enters the ear canal, it bounces around your pinna and produces echoes. So, for instance, sound coming from straight in front of you will have a different echo pattern than from a sound directly behind you. By covering your ears, you muffled the effect of those ridges and folds. In this experiment you discovered how good your ability is to locate things using only hearing. The next experiment really puts that ability to the test.

SCIENCE
Giants

Allesandro Volta, after whom we named the volt, made great contributions to the study of electricity. He was also interested in hearing, and set out to show that the hearing sense involved electricity. In 1790 he stuck a rod into each ear and zapped himself *with 50 voltas*! He said he felt a blow on the head followed by the sound of boiling water (his brain perhaps?), and concluded that hearing really does involve electricity. We now know that hearing, and all other senses, involves electricity, but it is in the range of *microvolts*! I have no idea what happened to him after this wacky experiment. Needless to say, you will never try anything this dangerous or dumb!

LET'S DO it!

Usually, where we *hear* something to be is also where we *see* it to be. For example, the chatter coming from your talking friend, *looks and sounds* as though it is coming from her mouth. But when the sound is not coming from where we see it, vision usually wins. We actually *hear* it coming from where we *see* it. This is called visual capture — as though vision "captured" the hearing sense, and it explains ventriloquism. Ventriloquists do not have any special knack to "throw their voices." No one can do that! Rather, if you hear a voice and see only the dummy's mouth moving, your brain assumes that is where it is coming from. Build and test this next gadget and discover how powerful visual capture is.

What You Need

at least 1.5 metres of tubing (large aquarium tubing is inexpensive—usually less than a dollar for this amount, and read the instructions below to figure out how much you need)

4 funnels (The narrow end should fit snugly into the tubing, the wide end should fit over your whole pinna. Flexible funnels are best)

a cap or toque
tape
elastic bands
needle and thread
cotton wool or soft foam
several friends

What To Do

1 Cut the tubing in half and firmly fit the funnels into each end.

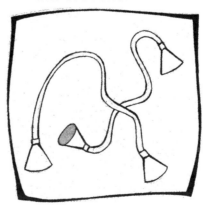

2 Join two funnels with elastic bands so that when placed over each ear they stay snugly in place. Take them off and glue a thick layer of cotton or foam around the wide end of these funnels. When dry, put them back on.

3 Tape the loose funnels to the funnels on the opposite ears. Have these funnels point out away from your head.

Ventriloquists are no Dummies

4. Sew the tubing to the hat in a few places. Do not puncture the tubing! Congratulations, you have just made a "Pseudophone" (SOO-doe-fone), which means "false sound."

5. Close your eyes. Have your friends scatter around you, and while wearing the pseudophone, listen to them talk and point to each friend as you call out his or her name.

6. Now open your eyes. Have your friends scatter around you and, while wearing the pseudophone, listen to them talk and pay attention to where each voice really *sounds* as though it is coming from.

Not surprisingly, since your ears have been "switched," with your eyes closed you probably always pointed in the opposite direction of the person you called out. But, amazingly, with your eyes open the voices really *sounded* as though they came from where you *saw* them. Why does the brain believe vision more than hearing? Probably because, normally, sounds *DO NOT* always come from their sources—think about echoes. Also, because light travels so much more quickly than sound, vision tells the brain exactly when and where something is happening, whereas sound can be incorrect. Think about seeing lightning but hearing the thunder afterwards, or think about the difficulty you had finding a jet plane way up in the sky whose sound was nowhere near its real location. Your brain chose to believe your eyes, not your ears.

Silent Sounds?

We cannot hear all vibrations. When you were born, you could probably hear down to 20 Hz and up to 20,000 Hz. (Frequency is measured in Hz, short for Herz. For example, 27 Hz is the lowest key on a piano, and 4186 Hz is the highest.) As we grow older, the range shrinks, especially at the high end. We cannot hear "sounds" outside this range.

The range of frequencies that other animals can hear is also limited. Take a close look at this graph. Do you notice anything odd? That's right, where the range falls is related to the size of the animal. Usually, the larger the animal is, the lower is its range. The range of tiny bats, for example, is way above and almost totally beyond the human range. Bats can hear up to 100,000 Hz! Elephants and blue whales can hear frequencies way below our range, down to 5 Hz!

This relationship between size and hearing range is not just a coincidence. Bats have tiny basilar membranes, and tiny membranes just cannot vibrate at low frequencies. Elephants and whales have huge basilar membranes (many times larger than a whole bat), and huge membranes just cannot vibrate very fast. What is *very* interesting is how these animals have taken advantage of their limited ranges. Bats navigate at night and catch insects using echolocation; they send out super-high frequency chirps and locate the echo. High frequencies

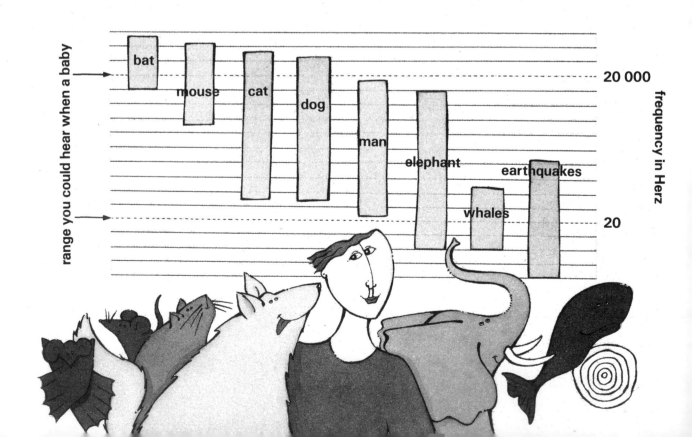

make perfect echoes off hard surfaces such as cave walls and insects. Low-frequency waves pass right around or through them. This is where the elephants come in. Elephants have a special knack that scientists have watched for at least a century, but could not explain until the mid 1980s. Elephants that are miles apart often do the exact same thing at the exact same time; herds will freeze, perk their ears and turn their heads to one side, then the other; herds miles apart can meet at some location and never go off course; mother elephants can directly find their baby in distress. They do this without the sense of smell, without vision, and without sound that we can hear. As you might have figured, elephants communicate in the subsonic range—frequencies below our range, as low as 5 Hz. They produce and hear "sounds" that are silent to us that can travel very long distances—miles in fact! Next time you are at the zoo, hang around the elephants for a while. You will not be able to hear their sounds, but your skin may feel them! Somehow, I think that if I lived in an earthquake zone, having a pet elephant would make a lot of sense. You figure out why (*Hint:* Go back to the graph).

ART & Science

Have you ever experienced a ringing in your ear? It is called Tinnitus (TIN-ih-tus) and in some people it is permanent and is enough to drive them really insane. You probably have heard of the brilliant but crazy Dutch artist Vincent van Gogh (pronounce the "gh" like a dog coughing up a hairball) who lived in the 19th century. You might also know that he sliced off most of his right ear with a razor. Some people think he did this simply as an act of pure craziness. Others also admit that he was crazy, but that he cut off the ear to stop the loud, constant tinnitus that he suffered. Unfortunately for poor Vincent, the ringing came from inside the ear.

OVER
100 Billion
Nerve Cells

The Sensory Brain

The different sense cells all over your body pick up different kinds of information and tell the brain about it. For example, your ears sense vibrations and your brain knows whether the sound is a car starting or someone whistling, as well as exactly where it is coming from.

Your brain constantly wants information about what is happening. During every second you are awake, your brain's billions of nerve cells receive information through millions upon millions of nerves from all over your body. (When you are asleep, your brain does not shut down. Some scientists think sleep is the time the brain does some housekeeping, such as organizing and

remembering the important things that happened during the day. The brain calms your body down so you do not harm yourself. While your brain is semi-disconnected

from your body, it concentrates on these other duties.)

Obviously, to handle so much information of all different kinds, the brain must

be very well organized. This diagram shows where information from some of the senses first ends up in the brain. The whole brain is made up of three parts.

The Hindbrain has the job of controlling basic things such as breathing, heart rate, sleeping and waking, and to coordinate your movements.

The Midbrain is the part where all the senses first connect to the brain and then pass on to other areas. The main job of the midbrain is to control your emotions, to guide your behaviour, and to control the level of alertness in different parts of the brain.

The Forebrain is the largest and most complicated part. The part that is most obvious is the curly-looking top, called the cortex. This is the part in which you experience things and think. For example, you use this part of your brain for vision and hearing, and for making difficult decisions and solving problems. If a sense does not connect here and have its own area, you do not experience the feeling directly.

The cortex has a left and right half. The left half controls the right side of your body and the right cortex controls the left half of your body. But the right and left half know what each is doing because they are connected by a huge cable with millions of nerves.

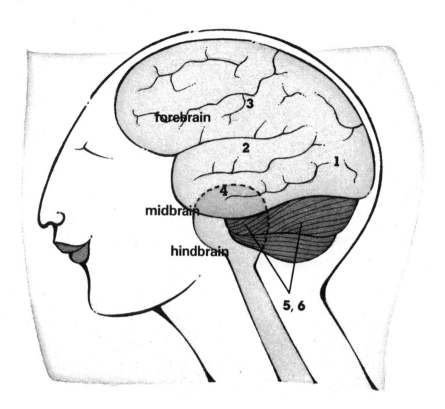

1 Vision

This is the largest area of the brain "owned" by any sense. It lies at the back and curves upward and to either side. Here is where the signals from the retina are broken down into edges of different sizes, tilts, and motions. These signals go to neighbouring visual areas where more information is organized. The layout of the visual world is preserved here in a map—the fovea is at the very tip of the visual cortex, and spreads around out to the periphery.

2 Hearing

The signals from the cochlea (inner ear) end at this large fold in the cortex. (This fold is like your thumb beside your fist.) The different frequencies, or speeds of vibrations, are laid out in a map just as they are in the ear. Low frequencies lie at the top of the fold, and high frequencies run down into the fold. Neighbouring areas make sense of the simple tones this area receives. In most of us, the right hearing cortex is where we hear music, and the left is where we make sense of speech.

3 **Touch** (pressure, hot, cold)

Lying along this side of the crack is where most of the different touch nerves end up. The nerves from different parts of your body have an order in a map. On the other side of the crack is the motor cortex, which controls how you move. Its map is just like the one along the touch cortex. This makes good sense—the brain does not have to look too far to find out how to move the part that was just touched. All parts do not occupy the same area: for instance, the skin on your shins and back have a small space, but your hands and lips occupy a huge space. And, you guessed it, that also explains why the mouth is so much more sensitive than the back.

4 **Smell and Taste**

No one completely understands the pathway of the signals from our taste buds and smell cells to the brain. We know they go to the midbrain (in fact, to that part that controls our feeling of hunger), and from there a few taste signals go on to the mouth part of the touch cortex. It may be that the midbrain does most of the smelling and tasting: babies born without a cortex make a "sour" face just as normal babies do when they are given a drop of lemon juice. On the other hand, adults with a damaged cortex may have trouble smelling and tasting, so the cortex must be involved somehow!

DID YOU EVER Wonder?

How many brain cells—neurons—do you actually have right now? That question is hard to exactly answer for any particular person. However, we do know there are a number of factors involved, such as your age and lifestyle practices (i.e. your consumption of alcohol and drugs). You had the greatest number of neurons when you were born—over 100 billion (that's 100,000,000,000)! But that total declines after birth by widely varying amounts in each person. Obviously intelligence doesn't depend on the number of neurons in the brain: newborn humans, in spite of their large number of neurons, function at a level way below the potential suggested by the number of brain cells they possess.

⑤ Body Sense
(muscle, joint)

The signals from all your muscles and joints go to the midbrain and to the hindbrain. The hindbrain has a special tangerine-sized part tucked under the visual cortex called the cerebellum (ser-ah-BELL-um). Its main job is to coordinate your movements and your posture. The simple act of raising your arm and pointing your finger requires the coordination of information coming from and going to many muscles and joints. The cerebellum makes sure each muscle does the right thing at the right time based on what the body senses are telling it. So far, it seems that there is no place in the cortex devoted to the body sense. That probably explains why we are not aware of it.

⑥ Balance Sense
(gravity, rotation)

The signals from the balance system also go to the midbrain and the cerebellum. In the cerebellum, your balance, body, vision and touch senses work together to coordinate your motions

DID YOU EVER
Wonder?

Intelligence depends, not on the number of neurons, but on the number of connections between them. Newborn brains have "loose" connections with only a few other neurons. Connections seem to grow in strength and in number the more you "exercise" that group of cells. Totally unused neurons seem to shrivel and disappear forever. So, to give one very simple example, if during your very early life, your visual system never experienced horizontal lines, no "horizontal" neurons would have developed, and you would be blind to horizontal things, such as venetian blinds, telephone lines, and the horizon. This may seem weird, but such people exist! Now sit back and imagine the billions of connections that are made and unmade every day in a baby's brain as it experiences the world. These connections ultimately "shape" the brain into its adult form. It is estimated that some single adult neurons may connect with over a thousand other neurons. You can think of the neurons themselves as our computer "hardware" and the kinds of connections, the computer "software." We humans are different because no two have identical experiences, so no two have the same software.

and posture. No one has yet found any place on the cortex for balance. That is why we do not feel balance the way we feel some other senses. But we do know that balance signals must connect to almost all the other senses, because of all the sensations we feel when we are unbalanced or dizzy.

The different senses use various parts of the brain, but these areas are also connected. Your senses usually work together to get the information your brain needs, and you saw many examples in this book of how one sense can affect another. Of course, this is not all that happens in the brain. After all, we do not just hear separate meaningless sounds. Instead, we hear music, words and sentences and thousands of other noises that we can identify. We do not just see patterns of light, of different greys and colours, but we see objects doing things, and animals and people we recognize—our pets, our grandmas and grandpas. In other words, the brain organizes these simple sensations and figures out what they *mean* as a whole and how we should act. Exactly how this happens is still a mystery. But we are sure that is what the whole brain is for.

Glossary

acuity   The smallest distance between two points before they blend into each other and seem like one point; as in visual acuity or touch acuity.

adaptation   Getting used to something. Once you have adapted, you are less sensitive than usual for a short time. All the senses adapt.

aftereffect   One event had an effect on sensation of a second event. Aftereffects can occur in all senses.

afterimage   The image that lasts a short time after you looked at something bright, or at something for a long time.

amplitude   The amount of vibration of a sound source or the waves it produces. You hear amplitude as loudness.

astigmatism   A focusing problem when the eye blurs lines of one tilt more than the opposite.

basilar membrane   A tissue sheet that divides the cochlea in half along its full length, and contains the hair cells. It vibrates in different places depending on the pitch of the sound.

citronellal   A manufactured pheromone that repels biting insects.

cochlea   The snail-shaped tunnel in your skull that has the hair cells that turn air vibrations into signals, which the brain translates into "sound."

cones   The light-sensitive cells in the eye that are found mostly in the fovea; they see best during the day, and take part in colour vision.

cornea   The clear bump on the front outside of your eyes, which does most of the light-bending to form an image on the back of the eye.

cupula   The "swinging door" of hair cells in the semicircular canal, which signals the direction the head is rotating.

Doppler Shift   The name for what happens when a vehicle passes you at a constant speed, but its pitch drops the moment it passes you.

ear canal   The hole in the middle of your pinna.

Eustachian tube   The tube that connects your middle ear to your throat.

evaporation   The process of molecules leaving a liquid to become a gas or vapour.

fovea   The central part of the retina that you use when you look at something. It has the best acuity, but only sees in daylight. It tells the brain what the image is.

frequency   The speed of vibration of a sound source or the waves it produces. You hear frequency as pitch. Frequency is measured in Herz (Hz); the number of vibrations in one second.

inertia   The idea that all things want to stay as they are. Moving things keep moving. Stationary things want to stay still.

kinesthesis   The system of senses in our muscles and joints that tells the brain where our body parts are and where they are moving.

lens   The lens fine-tunes the images at different distances from the eye to bring them into exact focus on the retina.

molecules   The tiny pieces of which all matter is made.

nasal cavity   The chamber just below each eye that contains the smell cells that detect odors breathed in through the nostrils.

nasal cycle   The regular switching between the nostrils in the breathing strength that occurs every two to three hours.

otoliths   The "ear stones" that allow the utricle to signal gravity.

periphery   All of the retina around the fovea. It helps you see where something is so you can swing your eye around to put the image on the fovea. It has poor acuity, but sees well at night.

pheromone   A chemical produced by insects and animals for communication. Different pheromones have different meanings.

pinna   The outer part of the ear that you can see.

retina   The complicated network of 128 million rods and cones and other cells that line the back of the eye and carry the pattern of the image to the brain.

rods   The light-sensitive cells in the eye, which are found mostly in the periphery, see best at night, and take part in seeing black and white.

semicircular canal   One organ of balance designed to tell the brain how the body is rotating. There are two (one behind each ear) for each of the three dimensions of space (3D).

stereogram   A pair of pictures of one scene that copies the two views seen by each eye. When they are combined in a stereoscope, you see in 3D.

stereoscope   A gadget that shows a different image to the right and left eyes. The result is simulated 3D vision.

stereovision   Seeing in three dimensions by combining into one, the two slightly different views from each eye.

utricle   One of the two organs of balance. The utricle tells the brain the direction of the pull of gravity which, in turn, indicates how your head is tilted.

Vomit Comet   The plane used by NASA to simulate near-zero-gravity on Earth.

Acknowledgements

Dr. Ken Money and Dr. Bob Cheung, Defence and Civil Institute
of Environmental Medicine Canada

Alison Pinsent, Health Protection Branch, Health and Welfare Canada

John Jenkins, General Mills Canada Inc.